MEDICAL PRACTICE MANAGEMENT
Body of Knowledge Review

3rd Edition

ORGANIZATIONAL GOVERNANCE AND PATIENT- CENTERED CARE

VOLUME 4

MGMA
104 Inverness Terrace East
Englewood, CO 80112-5306
877.275.6462
mgma.org

Medical Group Management Association®

Medical Group Management Association® (MGMA®) publications are intended to provide current and accurate information and are designed to assist readers in becoming more familiar with the subject matter covered. Such publications are distributed with the understanding that MGMA does not render any legal, accounting, or other professional advice that may be construed as specifically applicable to individual situations. No representations nor warranties are made concerning the application of legal or other principles discussed by the authors to any specific factual situation, nor is any prediction made concerning how any particular judge, government official, or other person who will interpret or apply such principles. Specific factual situations should be discussed with professional advisors.

Library of Congress Cataloging-in-Publication Data
Organizational governance and patient-centered care.
    p. ; cm. -- (Medical practice management body of knowledge review (3rd edition) ; volume 4)
    Includes bibliographical references and index.
    ISBN 978-1-56829-479-7 (alk. paper)
    I. MGMA (Association), issuing body. II. Series: Medical practice management body of knowledge review (Third edition) ; v. 4.
    [DNLM: 1. Practice Management, Medical--organization & administration--United States. 2. Patient-Centered Care--United States. W 80]
    R728
    610.68--dc23
                          2015025467

Item: 8823
ISBN: 978-1-56829-479-7

Printed in the United States of America

10 9 8 7 6 5 4 3 2

Body of Knowledge Review Series — Third Edition

Contents

Part 1

Organizational Governance

::: Introduction

Managing the governance of the medical practice organization is a centerpiece of the practice administrator's job. From maintaining required corporate documents, to participating in board of director or governing committee meetings, to fostering a culture of respect and trust, the practice administrator is the day-to-day caretaker of the organization's governance structure as well as its vision and mission. Part I of this volume follows the blueprint designed by practicing medical practice executives to describe the key competencies, knowledge, and skills required to develop and maintain effective organizational governance in the medical practice.

The major areas of competence in organizational governance, as identified by the certified and fellow members of the Medical Group Management Association, are facilitating the corporate legal structure and the governance for the organization and integrating the corporate mission, vision, and values statement into the organization's culture.

Within Chapters 1 and 2, these major competencies are further delineated according to the key knowledge and skills required to demonstrate competency as a manager of organizational governance. Examples of these supporting skills are maintaining adherence to corporate bylaws and required records; planning effective succession; and upholding the organization's mission, vision, and values.

Chapter 1

Organizational Governance and Corporate Structure

Organizational governance is important to all businesses. The modern medical group is no exception and, in a sense, is in greater need for focused attention to this topic as healthcare comes under ever-increasing scrutiny. Rising costs, medical errors and other quality concerns, changing revenue structures, potential conflicts of interest, and spiraling technology costs all create the need for increased attention to corporate structure and governing policies.

The key knowledge and skills necessary to effectively manage the corporate structure of a medical practice include:

- Knowledge of
  - Legal structures and effect on organizations;
  - Organizational policy and procedures;
  - Types of committees within a governance structure, including finance, personnel, quality review, research, recruiting, performance, and ad hoc; and
  - Board composition and procedural rules.
- Skill in
  - Defining the mission and vision of the organization;
  - Defining organizational bylaws;
  - Supporting the governing body in the development of a committee structure to meet the needs of the organization;

- Documenting the roles and responsibilities of the board of directors and committees;
- Maintaining adherence to and annual reviewing of corporate bylaws;
- Providing orientation and ongoing training for board and committee members;
- Documenting and retaining records;
- Maintaining organizational history;
- Participating in board and committee meeting management and board evaluation; and
- Planning effective succession.

::: Current Challenges in Corporate Structure

Medical practices today are dealing with a dynamic and diverse population. Expectations are high, and medical groups, like all healthcare organizations, must respond with better performance. The strategic direction of performance in a complex organization, such as a medical practice, is the responsibility of governance through the management of the intricate interrelationships of all of its members and stakeholders.

As groups increase in size, they also increase in diversity of thought, personality, and perspective, and there is a pressing need for new skills and knowledge in the areas of:

- Correct selection of group members;
- Policy and procedure;
- Leadership and governance; and
- Attention to organizational dynamics and a functional culture that places value on what advances the organization's mission.

::: Committee Structure

An essential element of governance is the delegation of tasks and duties for the group. The principal governing body may decide, as allowed or even required by the group's bylaws, to develop a committee structure that addresses operational concerns and process within the group in conjunction with the administration. This is a great way to provide physician input in a structured instead of ad hoc manner. It also provides a great opportunity to develop future leaders by educating them in the committee process and its importance.

Some of the more common committees within the governance structure are:

- Finance;
- Personnel;
- Technology;
- Quality review;
- Management (usually in smaller groups);
- Research;
- Recruiting;
- Education;
- Managed care;
- Medical practice development;
- Performance; and
- Ad hoc committees for many purposes, such as strategic planning, new construction, service-line development, and contract review.

Creating an Executive Committee in a Medical Practice

Going through the process of creating the executive committee must include approval from a majority of stakeholders. It is doubtful that this type of change will be unanimous, although that is certainly preferred. Even though the concept is formally approved, board members will look for ways to revert back to the old form of governance. The executive committee should be consistent and firm and remind the board that this change was approved by the shareholders and there is an expectation of support.

Building effective physician leadership is a work in process. It is helpful to encourage the physician and administrator to attend joint conferences on management and leadership subjects with expenses being paid by the medical practice. In addition, there are conferences specifically focusing on physicians in leadership roles, which will also be beneficial in building a strong physician–administrator team. The strength of the executive committee will help the board govern the medical practice effectively.

Executive committee responsibilities include operational, financial, and board-assigned tasks, as well as preparing the agenda for and running board meetings.

Daily Operational Issues

Daily operational issues can be dealt with in the following ways:

- The administrator will keep the executive committee informed about personnel, financial, or operational issues.

- Decisions regarding these issues shall be made by the executive committee, administrator, or brought to the board as appropriate.

- The administrator or the executive committee may establish ad hoc committees for special projects, such as recruiting.

Financial Health

The executive committee oversees the financial health of the medical group practice by:

- Focusing on financial opportunities for the medical practice (both revenue enhancement and cost reduction);

- Preparing annual operating and capital budgets;

- Overseeing compensation philosophy and benefits;

- Monitoring retirement plan, such as 401(k), performance;

- Assessing and recommending investments in new programs and services from a financial perspective;

- Developing and managing debt strategy;

- Recommending the timing and amount of quarterly shareholder bonuses to the board of directors; and

- Presenting next year's budget at the annual retreat.

Tasks Assigned by the Board

The executive committee also carries out any tasks assigned to it by the board by gathering information and providing complete analyses on board-referred projects.

::: Focus of Group Activities

Governing also needs to be concerned with the focus of group activities. Activities need to be grouped with consideration for function and customer interaction. In addition, leadership must be empowered to implement and act upon the governing board's policies and decisions. Typically this would mean the group should focus on three areas of oversight:

1. Internal functions;
2. External functions; and
3. Operations.

Regular reports to the board, as well as benchmarking these activities, can be very useful for the effective governance of the organization. It is also important to understand how these activities interact. This interaction has to be governed carefully to prevent a *silo* mind-set or *group think* from emerging.

::: Choosing an Appropriate Corporate Legal Structure

Business enterprises, including healthcare providers, use a variety of organizational forms as the legal structure for their activities. Their choice is based on how the structure provides legal and tax advantages and liability protection, and how it fits with the medical practice's overall business and professional strategic goals.

It is important to understand the legal structures of the medical practice for liability and taxation issues. Most medical groups in the United States take one of the following legal forms:

- Sole proprietorship or solo practice (with no separate legal entity);
- Professional corporation (PC) or professional association (PA);

- Professional limited liability partnership (PLLP); or

- Professional limited liability company (PLLC).

State laws regarding corporations and other forms of legal entities define the benefits and requirements of each of these structures. Medical practices are typically organized and operated through the use of a separate legal entity (e.g., a separately incorporated professional corporation) to shield the practice's owners' assets from any of the liabilities of the practice. This shield of *limited liability* is available, to differing degrees, under state laws allowing for the creation and use of PCs, PLLCs, and PLLPs. Few medical practices use a general partnership or limited partnership form of organization, primarily because these legal structures do not provide enough protection from liability.

From a tax perspective, the federal Internal Revenue Code and the Internal Revenue Service (IRS) also define how each of these legal structures are treated. For example, the IRS lets professional corporations be taxed the same as any other corporation (via C corporation tax treatment). Some professional corporations with only a limited number of members can select S corporation status, which allows the entity to be taxed as a partnership.

Physicians are always encouraged to seek legal advice prior to selecting a particular form of business entity for a medical practice. An attorney and an accountant should be consulted before deciding which form of entity to choose. Different legal forms have different benefits and burdens, and the best choice will depend on the medical practice's specific circumstances and goals. Many medical practices use the PC form of entity, although an increasing number of practices are forming PLLCs or PLLPs.

When choosing legal counsel, physicians typically select healthcare firms experienced in forming medical groups. Other physicians and the state and county medical societies can provide recommendations. The characteristics of common legal structures follow.

Sole Proprietorship

A sole proprietorship is a business with a single owner that is not established as a separate entity. In this structure, the assets of the individual physician and the medical practice are not separate, so the physician is not shielded from liability as he or she would be if a PC or similar structure was formed.

Some solo practices are organized in the form of PCs or similar legal entities owned by a single physician. Under such a structure, the physician is able to work in a solo practice format while obtaining the benefits of the shield of limited liability offered by using the corporate form. The advantages of a sole proprietorship include:

- Control — The physician-owner has total control over money and decisions because there are no partners or shareholders;

- Flexibility; and

- Ease of setup and management — A sole proprietorship is relatively easy to set up and requires no separate tax filing.

The disadvantages of a sole proprietorship include:

- No history for lending purposes — It is sometimes difficult for a new medical practice to borrow funds if it has no collateral;

- No backup — No one else can see patients when the sole proprietor is on vacation or is incapacitated for any reason and the cash flow stops;

- Full liability — In a true sole proprietorship, the physician-owner, not a separate legal entity, is responsible for all liabilities of the medical practice; and

- Full responsibility — the physician-owner is responsible for all decisions.

Professional and Business Corporations

A PC is a legal entity that is separate from its owners. Some states call this a *professional association* or a *service corporation*. A PC has four characteristics:

1. Limited liability;

2. Continuity of existence;

3. Transferability of ownership; and

4. Centralized management.

The PC is viewed as a separate entity for liability and taxation purposes. A PC is generally subject to the same basic requirements and rules as any other business corporation, except that the professional corporation variant requires that only licensed professionals (e.g., physicians) may own an interest in the medical practice. This means, for example, that a nonphysician generally cannot be an investor in a physician's PC. Additionally, ownership can be transferred only to another licensed professional.

A business corporation is also a separate legal entity that limits the liability of its owners. Unlike a PC, however, a business corporation allows for outside investors as well as ownership by nonphysicians. Business corporations are common for general commercial business activities, but such a form is rarely used for medical practices because most state licensing laws restrict medical practice ownership to licensed physicians.

The advantages of corporations include:

- Limited liability — Shareholders or owners are not liable for the debts of the medical practice;

- Extra tax deductions — Because the corporation pays the benefits, items such as health and life insurance become tax-deductible expenses of the corporation; and

- Transferability — Ownership may be transferred to another licensed person or entity.

The disadvantages of corporations include:

- Profits are taxable — Corporate-retained earnings are taxed, although this can be avoided in many instances by selecting S corporation treatment for tax purposes; and

- More complex governance limits control — The legal form of a corporation requires a governance structure with a board and elected officers.

Professional Limited Liability Partnerships and Professional Limited Liability Companies

PLLPs and PLLCs provide different levels of legal protection or limited liability to the organization's owners. Both structures allow the profits from the limited liability partnership (LLP) or limited liability company (LLC) to be taxed as partnerships. This means there is no potential for double taxation of entity profits, as in the case of a corporate form.

Like corporations, under most state laws LLCs and LLPs must be organized as *professional* versions of these legal structures, restricting ownership in a medical practice to licensed physicians in most states.

The procedure for setting up these or other forms of organizations is defined by state law, although most require filing articles of organization or similar shareholder documents with the state.

The major advantage of LLCs and LLPs is limited personal liability. The medical practice is treated as a partnership for tax purposes, so income and losses are passed through to the owners and not subject to double taxation.

The disadvantages of LLCs and LLPs are numerous:

- More complex governance — It is more difficult to establish strong governance;

- Physicians are not employees — Physicians generally are not employees of PLLPs or PLLCs, so they usually are not entitled to the same benefits as found in a PC or similar structure;

- Different financial management — Both entities require financial management practices somewhat different from those found in the more common PC form; and

- Variable state laws — Not every state allows the creation or use of a PLLP or PLLC for medical practices.

Matching the Legal Structure to Your Group's Corporate Culture

One question that needs to be answered when considering a legal structure for a medical practice is the influence of that structure on the culture of the group and the governance system the group envisions. In other words, the legal structure of a group will affect the culture and operational nature of the group. Discussion with a healthcare attorney and other medical groups will allow participants to see what has worked for other organizations. Identifying governance challenges the organization does not have the capacity or culture to meet will avoid costly and time-consuming errors. Changing the legal structure is much more difficult than creating the correct format from the inception.

Corporate Record-Keeping

Corporate records are legal documents that must be maintained in accordance with pertinent state and federal laws and regulations, which may vary by state and jurisdiction. Accordingly, it is essential that the governance plan address retention, storage, and retrieval policies for business documents.

The primary responsibility for ensuring proper storage and retention should include a designated backup custodian if the process owner (e.g., the medical practice executive or physician owner or partner) is unavailable. The plan should also include a loss control process for electronic backup of important documents, such as partnership and shareholder agreements, employment contracts, equipment leases, and real estate records. Under most circumstances, it is prudent to retain a copy of important documents at a location physically distant from the primary storage location. This should prevent any type of disaster from destroying executed copies of significant information. Many organizations keep original documents for the length of the statute of limitations pertinent to the most likely allegations related to the document. Some records are evergreen, whereas others may be replaced by newer versions, as in the case of leases.

The types of documents that should be addressed in a governance plan include, but are not limited to, the following:

- **Articles of incorporation.** In addition to copies retained by the organization and the state of incorporation, a copy should be retained by corporate counsel.

- **Bylaws.** Original and current copies should be retained.

- **Bylaw changes and documentation.** A copy of previous versions of bylaws should be retained for documentation in case of litigation. In addition, it is prudent to keep redlined versions of approved changes to facilitate the tracking of changes.

- **Stock and/or outstanding shares.**

- **Minutes (board, committee).** At least two archive copies should be retained in segregated, secure locations.

- **Employment agreements (physician, administrator, others).** These should be retained in accordance with applicable statutes.

- **General ledger.** Copies of the general ledger should be kept in accordance with applicable tax laws. External accountants or auditors often maintain duplicate records.

- **Corporate history.** Records of corporate history should be retained indefinitely in some retrievable format.

- **Medical records.** Different regulations and statutes apply to the retention of patient medical, employee health, and Occupational Safety and Health Administration records. Patient medical records are generally retained in accordance with the statute of limitations for billing compliance and for bringing malpractice action defined by the individual state or payer contracts. Employee records must be retained in accordance with the type of employee health services and surveillance provided on site. For both types of records, the medical practice should confer with counsel familiar with the applicable statutes for record retention.

- **Physician credentials.** Physician credentialing records may be accessed, despite their presumed protection from discoverability, by a variety of sources: governmental entities, such as the Joint Commission on Accreditation of Healthcare Organizations; the physician, if ever denied privileges; or a plaintiff who may allege negligent credentialing. Given those potentialities, credentialing records should be maintained for the maximum duration of the statute of limitations for bringing action against the hospital or according to record retention statutes of the state, whichever is longer.[1]

- **National Practitioner Data Bank (NPDB).** NPDB queries and reports should be maintained with and for as long as other credentialing files. Litigation based on negligent credentialing and hiring, or alternatively, litigation alleging wrongful termination or denial of privileges that call into question reports to or from the NPDB, will likely be needed when claims for wrongful termination or negligent credentialing practices are filed.

- **Discovery documents on current litigation.** These documents are important throughout the litigation and appeals process. It is generally prudent to retain records for 7 to 10 years after litigation in the event that a related case emerges. Records will likely be retained by counsel, and extended retention may not be required if the records become part of court records submitted as evidence in a trial or court proceeding.

Keeping an Organizational History

Organizational culture is an extremely important aspect of medical practice governance. Of course, positive cultures need to be maintained, and any negative culture needs to become a more positive one. Culture can be maintained by a focus on those aspects that are desirable. Recording the history of the group can enhance positive culture maintenance and make its accomplishments known. Publishing the history of the group and its culture in newsletters and Websites is important.

Cultural icons, such as photographs, awards, news articles, and mementos that are symbolic of important events in the group's history, should be properly archived and/or displayed. Activities such as service awards emphasize the group's positive values, which reinforces the importance of such ideals to new employees and physicians.

By its very nature, tribal knowledge is passed between stakeholders by storytelling and relaying the group's mythology to younger members. This information points to what is meaningful to its members, not necessarily to archivists. Be careful to identify and remember the stories that roam the hallways. A great amount of value may be assigned to these traditions and history that we celebrate and share, which need to be recognized and remembered.

::: Bylaws

Like policies and procedures, bylaws are dynamic documents that require regular maintenance. Changes in corporate law may require amendments to the bylaws, so a general review of corporate documents should be completed at least annually with special attention being paid to those areas that may have been the subject of changes during the year.

The following questions should be considered as the bylaws and policies of the group are reviewed:

- Has the group changed any committee structures this year?
- Has the group changed any of its procedures on elections?
- Has the group added any new shareholders or have any departed? If so, was their stock exchanged according to the bylaws?

- Are the duties outlined for officers and directors still current?

- Are minutes of meetings recorded and was a quorum present when decisions were made?

- Were the key decisions made according to the bylaws and governance documents?

- Does the group do things differently today than it did in the past?

- Has the makeup of the governance changed enough to warrant reviewing changing the bylaws?

- Has state corporate law changed since the group's bylaws were last reviewed by legal counsel?

Administrators must protect the integrity of the bylaws because failure to act within the scope of the bylaws may cause legal action by aggrieved shareholders and unnecessary intergroup relationship concerns. It is wise to periodically review the requirements of the bylaws with the board so the board members fully understand their requirements. It is essential that new board members be oriented to and understand this material, and all applicable stakeholders must have access to the governance documents for reference.

⋮⋮ Working with Boards

A group's governance begins with a clear understanding of what the process of governance entails and what the role of governance is or should be in the medical practice. This includes extensive knowledge of how a board of directors works and what responsibilities its members have.

Board Responsibilities

The role of the board should be clearly understood. The responsibility of the board is mostly about relationship management, but there are some specific tasks involved with each board member's role, including:

- Developing the organizational mission;

- Providing and monitoring institutional goals;

- Taking responsibility for and ensuring the quality of care;

- Managing the relationship with the administrator of the group;
- Interacting with other leaders in the group;
- Managing relationships with the group's constituencies;
- Assessing and controlling quality;
- Keeping the health group fiscally sound (financial concerns);
- Implementing self-assessment and development; and
- Monitoring performance.

It is very important that every potential member of the board understand his or her role and the expectations of the job. For example, a prospective board member might read a job description similar to the sample shown in Exhibit 1.1.

In medical groups, most members of the board are physicians; although their duty is to the group as a whole, from time to time they may find it difficult to let their own interests or the interests of their specialty be secondary to the needs of the entire group.

Board Composition and Meeting Procedural Rules

Most times, board membership occurs via an election, and those election rules will be specified in the bylaws of the organization. It is imperative that the group's bylaws be properly adopted and that the procedures outlined in the bylaws are adhered to carefully. Failure to correctly follow the process could result in a challenge to the legitimacy of the process and invalidate actions under state law.

Board Evaluation

The board's prospective members need to be evaluated based on their performance of predetermined criteria that have been communicated clearly before an individual becomes a member of the board.

At least annually, the board should conduct a useful self-review of performance and provide feedback to the individual board members. This should include a checklist of board responsibilities. Evaluation of present board members could include the following:

- Board members must meet the attendance requirement. This is usually a high percentage of all meetings, often 75 percent.
- Board members must come prepared to meet and discuss the agenda items.

EXHIBIT 1.1

Sample Job Description

The ABC Medical Practice's Board Member
Job Description and Expectations

Purpose	To advise, govern, oversee policy and direction, and to assist with the leadership and general promotion of the practice so as to support the organization's mission and needs and to work closely with the administration of the practice in order to achieve its goals.
Number of Members	[Specify the number of members. The typical number is between 5 and 11, depending on the size of the group.]
Major Responsibilities	■ Organizational leadership and advisement ■ Organization of the executive committee officers and committees ■ Formulation oversight of policies and procedures ■ Financial management [to be defined] ■ Review and adoption of budget for the organization; review of quarterly financial reports; assist with administration with budgetary issues as necessary ■ Oversight of program planning and evaluation ■ Hiring, evaluation, and compensation of senior administrative staff ■ Review of organizational and programmatic reports ■ Promotion of the organization ■ Strategic planning and implementation
Length of Term	[Specify length of term, which may be staggered.]
Meetings & Time Commitment	[Specify the time and location of meetings such as, "The executive committee will meet every other Friday commencing at 7:30 a.m., and meetings will typically last one (1) hour (this may need to be revised)." An alternative would be to have monthly meetings (2 to 3 hours) in the afternoon or evening (consider payment to participants).]
Expectation of Board Members	■ Attend and participate in meetings on a regular basis and special events as possible. ■ Participate in standing committees of the board and serve on ad hoc committees as necessary. ■ Help communicate and promote mission and programs of the practice. ■ Become familiar with the finances and resources of the practice as well as financial and resource needs. ■ Understand the policies and procedures of the practice.

EXHIBIT 1.1   *(continued)*
Sample Job Description

The ABC Medical Practice's Board Member
Job Description and Expectations

Board and Committee Structure

Establishing Committees — It shall be the responsibility of the executive committee to establish ad hoc and permanent standing committees as necessary to assist in the functioning of the practice. Whenever possible, these committees should contain a representative of the executive committee to provide a proper liaison as well as an administrative staff person.

Typical Committees — [Include: finance, personnel, marketing, quality care, and technology. In areas where managed care risk contracting is a significant part of the business environment, a utilization management committee would be common to oversee the risk management of these contracts.]

- Board members should be evaluated on their expertise. What skills is each specific member asked to contribute? Is the member an expert in business operations, finance, marketing, or law? It is not uncommon for the group's legal counsel to attend board meetings. At least in theory, board meetings can be protected by attorney–client privilege when legal counsel is present.
- Board members must respect the confidentiality of the board's activities. They must also support the decisions of the board outside the boardroom.
- Board members must disclose conflicts of interest.
- Board members must show respect to management and its role to implement board policy.
- Board members must act in a prudent manner, provide fiduciary responsibility, and understand their behavior is representative of the group at all times.

Response to Stakeholders' Needs

The medical group's board must deal with a number of stakeholders in the quest to provide effective governance of the group. Some of these stakeholders are:

- Physicians in the medical group practice;
- Other physicians in the community;
- Employees;
- Patients, their families, and caregivers;
- Payers;
- Government agencies at the federal, state, and local levels;
- The community at large; and
- Hospitals and healthcare entities.

Management of Board Meetings

Most board meetings are governed by *Robert's Rules of Order*,[2] which is the most widely accepted set of procedures for conducting business. These rules are extensive and cover a number of procedures that apply to the medical group setting. Some, however, may not apply to every group's needs, although familiarity with *Robert's Rules* as a whole is important. Whatever system of rules the board decides to adopt, the goal is to apply the rules consistently.

Outside Board Members

Increasingly, medical groups are beginning to behave more like traditional business corporations. As part of this change, groups are adding outside persons to the board to improve the governance process and to bring in new ideas and perspectives. These individuals must be chosen carefully with consideration of a number of important criteria, including:

- A general understanding of the region, its business climate, political environment, and some of the key community drivers, as well as some perspective on healthcare and what is happening in the broad view;
- Strategic thinking;
- Willingness and ability to attend meetings;
- Ability to treat information discreetly;
- Some experience as a member of a board;

- No conflicts of interest or the appearance of such conflicts (e.g., not someone seeking to do business with the clinic);

- General business acumen;

- Contributing without dominating the board;

- A history of working well in a group setting (i.e., a good fit);

- Willingness to sign a confidentiality or nondisclosure agreement; and

- Willingness to accept fair compensation if applicable.

::: Conducting a Governance Self-Assessment

It is helpful before and after implementing the information in this book to assess how well your medical group handles governance. Numerous telltale symptoms begin to surface as a sign that your board of directors or executive committee may be functioning below the standards necessary for effective governance. To identify these signs and symptoms, each board member should assess these 10 core issues:

1. Are the appropriate subcommittees in place, including quality assessment, information technology (IT), operations, and finance? Or, do you find yourselves trying to address all of these topic areas at your monthly board meetings?

2. If you have subcommittees in place, do you routinely accept those committee recommendations without robustly analyzing and considering the key issues facing the organization?

3. Similarly, do you routinely accept the medical group practice administration's recommendations without rigorously considering and discussing them?

4. Do you spend most of your time at board meetings digging into operational matters without regard for the big picture?

5. How many agenda items represent board members' pet projects?

6. If one of your board members has sponsored an agenda item, do you have a process for analyzing these issues with that person in the room, and is your decision free from bias?

7. Do you have a process by which you provide training and continuing education to board members?

8. Do you have a process by which you orient and educate new board members?

9. Do new board members passively sit at the table and try to understand how the game is played, or do they actively participate in discussions and clearly understand what is expected of them?

10. Do you have a process by which you identify future board members and evaluate their performance through their service on subcommittees?

⠿ Corporate Decision Making

Getting everyone in a medical group to agree on everything is always a challenge, and part of organizational governance is finding ways to responsibly and legally make decisions.

The Decision-Making Process

The styles of decision making that naturally flow from the group's culture are as follows:

- **Directive style** is characteristically adopted when tolerance for ambiguity is low and the decision makers tend to be uncompromising and rational in their thinking. Minimal information is used and few alternatives are given for consideration.

- **Analytical style** is typical when there is a higher tolerance for ambiguity and decision makers are rational in their thinking. Decision makers typically give careful consideration to unique situations.

- **Conceptual style** is seen when there is a high level of ambiguity. Decision makers using conceptual style are intuitive rather than rational in their thinking.

- **Behavioral style** is evident when the decision maker wants to avoid conflict or places greater importance on social relationships and is receptive to suggestions.

Decision making has been studied in depth and there are two types of problems in corporate decision making: (1) well-structured or programmed problems, and (2) unstructured or unprogrammed problems.

Structured problems involve goals that are clear and are often familiar because they have occurred before. These problems are easily and completely defined with available information. Structured problems are usually programmed, repetitive, and can be handled by a routine approach. Decision rules can be developed and applied repeatedly. Such decisions can be easily delegated because the rules can be explained and assigned in advance and do not need to involve the group's governance structure.

Structured decisions can involve policies, procedures, and rules. *Policies* are general guidelines for making a decision about a structural issue, for example, "All employees receive 10 days of vacation after one year of service." A *procedure* is a series of interrelated steps that a manager can use to respond to a structure issue. For example, a manager may calculate the amount of vacation an employee receives the same way each time. *Rules* are explicit statements that limit what can or cannot be done to carry out a procedure. For example, a group could decide to prorate the amount of vacation for employees who do not work full time.

Ideally every challenge a medical group practice faces would be structured with a policy or procedure readily available to help guide the decision. In a medical practice, this is often not the case. Many times unstructured problems are more strategic in nature, such as when to add a new service or how to respond to a competitive change in the market. The strategic nature of unstructured problems often requires groups to use the formal governance structure to make decisions.

::: Change-Agent Management

Medical practice executives must lead, not just manage. Management and leadership, however, are often confused with one another. Management's role is to implement the policies and execute the strategies determined by the governing body. The governing body will allocate resources for implementation, but it is the practice manager's responsibility to determine how the strategy is implemented. Implementation is not the function of the governing body, although this lack of distinction is frequently seen in the medical practice setting.

Members of the governing body must be leaders. To answer the question, "How do leaders lead?" consider some of the absolute requirements of leadership. Leaders:

- **Interpret reality** in an understandable way;
- **Explain the present** in clear and factual terms; and
- **Paint a picture of the future** using a compelling vision.

First, leaders must interpret reality in an understandable way. The current situation must be clear and unambiguous. This provides context for the actions needed to move the organization forward. Medical groups often are not fully aware of their current reality, or even how their surroundings (environment, patients, and the outside world) affect them, because of the lack of market surveillance with an eye to the future. They need to poll the community and be observant of changes.

This reality must be explained in ways that provide factual and actionable information, free of the emotion and judgment that often clouds the picture and turns the focus to argument, not action. Once this basis is established for the present, a compelling picture can be developed for future action. After all, who would want to follow a leader who has little to offer in the future or little to say about that future? A big part of leadership is the motivation to act. People have to believe in the vision of the future. They must want to see it happen, and they must want to be part of that future.

Trust

An essential element for the governance of a medical practice is trust, partnered with its development and maintenance. Trust interrelationships within the medical group are numerous and interdependent, as shown in Exhibit 1.2.

A cornerstone in the readiness to change is trust. Conversely, the failure to change is often caused by a lack of trust. Trust comes in many forms, including authentic, naïve, and blind.

Authentic trust is earned over a period of time. *Naïve trust* — a sort of natural trust — is given without being earned. *Blind trust* is similar to naïve trust; trust is given because there is no reason *not* to trust the other party. Blind trust can be based on reputation or other factors.

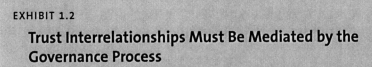

EXHIBIT 1.2

Trust Interrelationships Must Be Mediated by the Governance Process

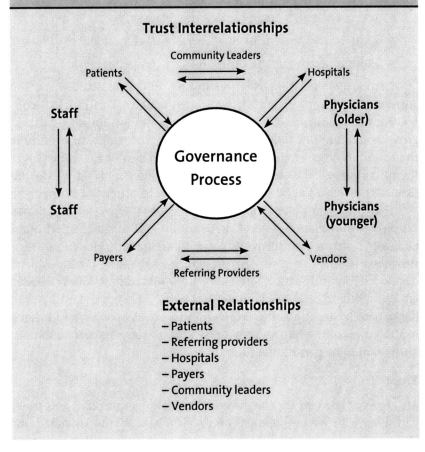

The primary factor causing loss of trust is a sense of deception. It is essential in the medical group to preserve and, at times, regain trust by carefully communicating the following:

- Facts that have been carefully checked for accuracy;

- Quick admission of all mistakes; and

- Full disclosure in situations, so a lack of trust is not created when there is a perception of providing only part of the story.

Such communications should become a natural part of the interaction between group members. Trust is established and maintained by consistent patterns of behavior.

::: Succession and Replacement Planning

Succession planning and replacement planning are necessary components of the strategic plan and the disaster management plan for every medical practice. They are critical components for business continuity. Succession planning is a long-term strategic tool, and replacement planning is a short-term disaster management tool. Both are used in response to the loss of key employees and providers. Some of the early preparation components are similar, but the processes differ significantly as they progress.

The need for succession and replacement plans is urgent, as a 2011 study by the American Management Association shows that fewer than 7 percent of healthcare organizations are seen as well prepared to deal with the sudden loss of key leaders.[3]

Key Employees

Before creating a succession or replacement plan, it is important to know who and what is involved. One factor is key employees. *Key employees* are individuals who hold a leadership position or an employee who is the only employee performing a key role within an organization.

There are many titles for key employees. In a medical practice, these may include the administrator, practice manager, clinical manager, billing manager, front office coordinator, and IT manager. The administrative assistant who performs multiple tasks may also be a key employee. Each one performs job duties that are essential for the practice to be successful. To identify the key employees in a practice, Paul Sullivan, a consultant for Olmstead & Associates, suggests the following questions:[4]

- Who are the most valuable employees in my office? Do they operate independently performing undocumented procedures?
- What would happen to the practice if, from this moment on, I never see them again?
- What would I need to do to return to normal without them?

Succession Planning

Succession planning is the process of ensuring that a business will continue operating by defining key roles and competencies, identifying individuals within the organization to take over key positions, and then developing those individuals' knowledge and skills to allow for seamless transitions.[5] This planning is proactive. The owner of a business, or the lead physician, is usually the subject of succession planning, and the topic is usually addressed near retirement age or during the final segment of a leadership term in the office.

Succession planning is an orderly, staged replacement process for senior leaders. It lets an organization continue to operate regularly after the loss of a key employee.[6] Succession planning should be discussed by the organization's board, and the board should have a team or individual accountable for the process. As part of the strategic plan, it establishes systems that make it possible for the organization to go on, as best as possible, when a key individual leaves.

It is extremely risky to wait until an employee reaches retirement age to begin this process. The sudden loss of a key employee because of other employment, health issues, or a life-altering injury may force the practice to proceed with replacement planning and may jeopardize practice operations.

Effective planning for succession starts with the identification of key employee roles. Then the operational pieces have to be put into place. Job analyses, job descriptions, and job specifications have to be developed for each position. These will be discussed more in detail in the section on replacement planning, but they need to be updated at least annually, especially in a medical practice where new regulations frequently alter the way business is performed. Once the paperwork is completed, the recruitment process begins with the consideration of possible candidates. The practice should let internal staff members know if they are being considered for succession, and if so, they should be invited to participate in the development process.

Development Process

The first part of the development process is an assessment of the candidate(s). Two or more individuals may be chosen to participate. The assessment process begins by asking the following questions of each candidate:

- Are you prepared to take on the responsibilities of the position?
- What additional formal training or education do you need?
- What can you be taught on the job?
- What is the time frame for development?

The next step is formal development and mentoring. If additional education is required, management should establish a timeline for this to be completed.

The individual(s) should begin working with a mentor immediately, who may or may not be the current key employee holding the position. This training period is crucial for a successful transition. Many organizations identify candidates for leadership positions and then provide no formal development. When the time comes to replace the key employee, the candidate(s) are no closer to assuming responsibilities than an outside hire.

In a medical practice, succession planning has historically involved only the physician(s). In a smaller physician practice, another physician may need to be recruited and groomed to take over the practice. In a larger practice, a physician partner may be chosen to be the future leader of the organization.

There may also be a rotation of physicians in the leadership position for multiple year terms. The succession process works best when there are two to three years of lead time.

While it is important to have this process in place for physicians, it is also wise to implement it with other key positions. Many medical practices are small businesses with fewer than 100 employees, and, therefore, it may not be possible to locate internal candidates for succession. Unfortunately, a successor with the education, skills, abilities, and personality that complements the culture of the practice may not be found within the practice.

If, however, the practice has been able to identify an individual who has the characteristics to fill the position from within, many uncertainties are eliminated. Succession planning is always preferable to replacement planning. Because the employee is in house, it is more likely that he or she has been provided with the necessary information and background to assume the position. The employee may have learned tips and tricks over the years. Passwords and log-ins are more likely to be handed over, as well as the locations of important files in the computer system and throughout the office. Important dates and deadlines, as well as passing on the knowledge of critical relationships, can be extremely valuable information for the survival and success of the medical practice. However, more often than not, the practice is forced to go through the replacement planning process rather than succession planning.

Replacement Planning

Replacement planning is reactive. This is the process of filling a position after it becomes vacant because of turnover.[7] There are numerous tasks to complete to determine the individuals to recruit. Replacement planning can be very challenging for a medical practice because of short notice, and these tasks should be reviewed and updated regularly to plan contingencies in preparation for losing key employees.

Replacement planning can be a protracted process. Good preparation helps immensely. Unfortunately, the likelihood that the practice has completed all of the preparation for replacement planning and kept it updated is low, thus leaving the company at a distinct disadvantage. The impact depends on how much time there is to prepare before the loss of the key employee.

The sudden loss of a key employee because of injury, health issues, or even death can have a tremendous effect on the practice. The mixture of emotions compounded by the effect of the loss of business operations can be debilitating. If replacement planning has not been completed, the leaders of the group will have to quickly determine what tasks performed by the key employee are crucial to business operations. These might be payroll, submitting patient claims, scheduling surgeries, or any number of other important office duties.

If cross-training has not occurred, and the tasks require software or other training, such as payroll and claims submission, vendors can be called and contracted for assistance. Online assistance may also be available. If passwords and log-ins are required and have not been located, place a call to the vendor's customer support and explain the situation. A request on company letterhead signed by a principal may be required to change the contact person on an account. Then it is time to search the files, e-mail, Internet favorites and bookmarks, desk drawers, and lockers. If this key employee was truly an independent worker, it may take some time to learn all of his or her regular tasks. In the meantime, the practice has to decide how to fill this position. Decisions will have to be made whether some or all duties will be allocated to other employees on a permanent basis, whether the job will remain as it was, or whether outsourcing will be a better option. The answer could be a combination of these.

Worst-Case Scenarios for Replacement Planning

Although the severe illness or death of a key employee can be distressing, the immediate dismissal of a key employee who has committed fraud or embezzlement can be devastating. Not only does the practice have to deal with finding a replacement employee, but many hours of work must be devoted to identifying and remedying problems while dealing with litigation. If Health Insurance Portability and Accountability Act privacy has been violated, additional work may be involved. This is very costly to a practice, in dollars and in public image. The absence of a completed replacement plan in this situation compounds all of the issues and can be very damaging to the practice.

Two other less devastating scenarios for losing key employees also exist. The first is a key employee who gives notice that he or she is leaving the practice. The time frame for this is usually two to four weeks, unless the company's policy is to terminate employment or accept the resignation immediately. Within those two to four weeks, management should initiate or review the replacement plan processes, giving them higher priority than usual. Cross-training on essential duties can be initiated and procedures can be written up. Contacts, passwords and log-ins, and other important files can be located, and copied if necessary. The exiting employee may be able to assist in developing the job analysis. The company will, once again, have the options of hiring for the same position, distributing some or all of the tasks among other employees, or outsourcing some or all of the work.

The last and often least devastating scenario is retirement. Ideally the practice will have significant notice for this event, but some individuals choose to make retirement an immediate event. To prevent this, conversations should be initiated asking the employee if he or she has any plans for retirement. Human resource consultants agree that introducing this topic of discussion between the ages of 55 and 60 is appropriate. If the significance for the practice knowing these plans earlier rather than later is communicated to the employee, adequate notice may be given to allow for replacement or even succession planning.

⁝ Conclusion

Effective management of organizational governance and corporate structure is a key component in building and sustaining a culture that supports the care delivery and financial health of the medical practice. Creating a corporate structure that provides solid guidelines to protect the interests of the stakeholders while providing enough leeway to act on new strategies is a delicate balance all administrators face.

Notes

1. K.S. Davis, J.C. McConnell, and E.D. Shaw, "Data Management," in *The Risk Management Handbook for Healthcare Organizations*, ed. R. Carroll (San Francisco: Jossey-Bass, 2004), 1220.

2. Robert, Henry M., *Robert's Rules of Order Revised* (Glenview, IL: Scott, Foresman, 1994).

3. American Management Association/Corporate Learning Solutions, "Study Sees Looming Crisis for Healthcare Leadership," *Medical Benefits* 28, no. 7 (Apr. 15, 2011): 10–11.

4. Paul Sullivan, "Protecting Your Firm Against Loss of Key Employees," *Illinois Bar Journal* (March 2002): 147.

5. Scott Ransom, "Succession Planning Is Vital New Skill for Physician Executives," *Physician Executive* 29, no. 2 (Mar/Apr 2003): 59.

6. Hildy Gottlieb, "Succession Planning: The Elephant in the Room," ReSolve Inc., 2006, http://policylinkcontent.s3.amazonaws.com/ARTICLE -Succession_Planning-The_Elephant_in_the_Room.pdf.

7. Leigh Richards, "Succession Planning vs. Replacement Planning," Demand Media, Inc., n.d., www.ehow.com.

Chapter 2

Change Management and Upholding Corporate Mission

Healthcare delivery organizations exist in an environment that is experiencing ever higher rates of change. Traditionally, these organizations have been quick to adopt medical technology but slow to embrace organizational change. One of the key contemporary focuses in organizational governance is the identification of the practice's corporate culture and the implementation of effective change management processes within that culture.

Although technology is useful, customer service and other human interactions define how the practice is perceived. Despite healthcare delivery addressing the most important and intimate aspects of the human condition, the industry has often failed to properly focus on relationships. It has become imperative for medical practices to address the quality of their relationships with all of their stakeholders, both internal and external.

The key knowledge and skills necessary to effectively integrate the corporate mission, vision, and values statements into the organization's culture include:

- Upholding the organization's mission, vision, and values through accountability;
- Providing leadership, innovative thinking, and change management;
- Upholding and advocating ethical standards, behavior, and decision making; and
- Fostering a culture of trust and respect.

Developing the vision, mission, values, norms, and short- and long-term goals is a critical step in building an aligned organization, but without fostering a culture of communication and accountability, a medical practice may not have clear purpose or direction. It is the duty of the administrator to make sure the mission, vision, and values are incorporated at the heart of daily operations.

⋮⋮⋮ Developing Values

Values answer the question: "What are the basic beliefs we share as an organization?" Strong values statements keep an organization on track by helping to foster the right choices in day-to-day and strategic decision making. Along with mission and vision, they provide the board, physicians, and staff members a foundation for addressing challenges, including financial crises and strategies to cope with changes in the environment. They help with difficult ethical questions that stray into gray areas. In periods of turbulence or change, values provide stability and a sense of purpose.

Developing meaningful values can be an important investment in an organization because strong values provide the foundation for the culture and can positively affect the recruitment, retention, and commitment of staff and patients. Leaders must know what they care about, because one can only be authentic when leading others according to the principles that matter most to one's self. If the leader's values are not the same as those of the organization, it is difficult to align performance with goals. Leaders who want to clarify their own values can ask themselves questions such as:[1]

- What do I stand for? Why?
- What do I believe in? Why?
- What causes me discontent? Why?
- What am I passionate about? Why?

Researchers have found that there are three central themes in the values of highly successful, strong-culture organizations:[2]

1. High performance standards;
2. A caring attitude toward people; and
3. A sense of uniqueness and pride.

Values in a medical practice can vary greatly depending on specialty, location, and socioeconomic standing of the community. Examples of key words used to express a practice value include commitment to excellent services, innovation, diversity, creativity, honesty, integrity, teamwork, trust, accountability, and continuous improvement.

::: Integrating the Mission Statement into the Practice Culture

One major consideration in strategic planning is the culture of the organization. Although there is not one standard definition of *organizational culture*, "the way we do things around here" is an efficient and frequently cited commonsense definition of *culture*.

Many of the problems confronting administrators can be traced to their inability to analyze and evaluate organizational cultures. When trying to implement new strategies or a strategic plan, medical practice executives will often discover that their strategies will fail if they are inconsistent with the organization's culture.

Schein[3] presents five guidelines for the administrator when addressing organizational culture:

1. Don't oversimplify culture or confuse it with climate, values, or corporate philosophy. Culture *underlies* and largely *determines* these other variables. Trying to change values or climate without getting at the underlying culture will be a futile effort.

2. Don't label culture as solely a human resource (read "touchy-feely") aspect of an organization, affecting only its human side. The impact of culture goes far beyond the human side of the organization to affect and influence its basic mission and goals.

3. Don't assume that the leader can manipulate culture just as he or she can control other aspects of the organization. Culture, because it is largely determined and controlled by the members of the organization, and not the leaders, is different. Culture may end up controlling the leader rather than being controlled by the leader.

4. Don't assume that there is a right or wrong culture, or that a strong culture is better than a weak one. It should be apparent that different cultures may fit different organizations and their

environments, and that the desirability of a strong culture depends on how well it supports the organization's strategic goals and objectives.

5. Don't assume that all the aspects of an organization's culture are important, or will have a major effect on the functioning of the organization. Some elements of an organization's culture may have little effect on its function, and the leader must distinguish which elements are important and focus on those.

An understanding of culture and how to transform it is a crucial skill for administrators trying to achieve strategic outcomes. Because of their position in the organization, administrators are best situated to see the dynamics of the culture, such as what should remain and what needs transformation. This is the essence of strategic success.

::: Accountability

Doing the right thing, regardless of consequences, is easier said than done, but in an industry where staff members deal with life and death, it is a goal worth achieving. By doing the right things consistently, leaders build accountability among staff members and diminish the temptation to use excuses.

The key to greater accountability starts with practice managers who help create and implement mission, vision, and value statements that should resonate with physicians' beliefs. Living those beliefs is the way to ensure that the practice culture aligns with the beliefs, and that staff understand those beliefs and act accordingly.

Small efforts and personal investments in staff make an important difference in medical group practices. Clear distinctions between good and bad behavior must be made in order to positively influence behaviors in the staff.

The best method to create a culture of accountability includes:

- Setting expectations with staff members;
- Communicating them clearly to employees;
- Delegating effectively; and
- Empowering staff members to execute independently.

People are responsible for things and accountable to people, and that accountability is tied to relationships, which — at their core — are about people helping people. For more accountability in the office, practice executives must start talking about what that word means to them. They must prove it through their actions and set expectations for staff members to emulate it.

::: Leadership Team Principles

The roles of physician and nonphysician leadership within the medical group will vary greatly from group to group, but certain principles should apply regardless of the group's size or structure. The best model is the physician–administrator executive team, in which a physician and practice executive work collaboratively to provide leadership to the group.

The tasks for the team dyad include:

- Development of policies, plans, and procedures;
- Licensing, compliance, and continued training;
- Quality assurance, monitoring, and organizational performance;
- Advisory role to the governing board;
- Staff development planning;
- Liaison for professional and nonprofessional staff;
- Interaction with patients, complaint resolution, and service recovery; and
- Interaction with outside groups and organizations.

How tasks are carried out and which leader performs each task will depend on how much time the physicians have for these duties, as well as their skill sets, experience, and attitude about the work.

Many groups do provide some so-called administrative time to physician leaders, and some large practices have full-time medical directors, but in most smaller groups, leadership and governance are voluntary activities or may be assigned to multiple individuals by the group.

Groups may have rotating physician leadership, which is intended to spread the responsibility in an egalitarian manner throughout the group. Such a plan, however, ignores the reality that leadership and effective governance are skills that must be learned, nurtured, and developed. Such an ad hoc approach also does not consider inherent leadership abilities, which some people lack and must be trained to develop.

Relationship building is fundamental to the successful team. In his book *The Five Dysfunctions of a Team*,[4] Patrick Lencioni talks about five clear and easily identifiable factors that prevent effective teamwork, whether it is a 2- or 20-person team:

1. Lack of trust;

2. Fear of conflict;

3. Lack of commitment;

4. Avoidance of accountability; and

5. Inattention to results.

A great team's members are business partners. They trust one another, communicate openly, and keep the best interests of the group in mind with all decisions. Above all, they offer each other respect and unconditional support. Someone who cannot support the team in an unconditional way needs to resign from the team, resolve the conflict behind closed doors, or accept a poorly performing team. The typical advocacy form of interaction is passé and useless for the transformation and development of the group; it only achieves the goals of one individual or a small group of individuals.

Team leadership can be described with the story of the buffalo and the geese. Buffalo Bill Cody discovered early in his legendary slaughter of these great beasts that he could effectively kill an entire herd by shooting the lead bull first. Once the lead bull dropped, the other animals became confused and they would stop, not knowing what to do, thereby becoming easy targets for the sharpshooters.

In contrast, a flock of geese flies in a V shape, not because of an artistic flair, but because it is efficient. By flying behind one another in formation, wind resistance is reduced and the most distance is covered with the least expenditure of energy. Of course, the lead goose is blazing the trail and eventually will get tired and drop back in the V, only to be replaced by another goose. This is a trait that any organization should strive to emulate. If one goose gets sick, they will all land, and another goose will accompany the sick goose until it dies or becomes well enough to proceed. Geese also honk, not to telegraph their location, but to encourage the goose in front of them to keep flying and to tell their leader, "we are behind you!"[5]

Team Goals

Running a successful medical practice requires a team of people who all share the same vision and all focus on the same direction. Teams can become dysfunctional for many reasons, including:

- Fuzzy measures and targets;
- Unclear strategies and weak top-management commitments;
- Gaps between organization goals and department goals, or department goals and individual team member goals; and
- Failure to connect individual or team accountabilities to rewards.

Research shows that less than 20 percent of employees know their organization's business strategy. Only two-thirds of vice presidents believe that their leadership team is in agreement on the business strategy. Consider the effect on employees and on an organization's ability to embed its strategic goals into department goals when less than 20 percent of the staff members are fully aligned. Recent research finds that 15 to 25 percent of workforce time is wasted on low- or no-value activities.[6]

Aligning every team member with the vision, mission, values, and goals is critical to success in all organizations, especially medical practices, where the health and wellness of patients is the goal.

Organizational goals are usually established for two to five years, and then short-term goals are set for one year. A key to successful goal-setting is for everyone on the team to accept and own the goals. When people actively participate in developing their goals, they become motivated to reach the target. Meetings are typically held to set goals. The number of meetings depends on the size of the organization. Only one goal-setting meeting may be needed for small organizations. Several meetings may be necessary to reach everyone in the organization — one with the practice management, another with department managers, and then others with team members.

These 11 steps can be followed for setting aligned goals:

1. Review your vision, mission, values, and norms.

2. Review long-term and short-term goals for the entire organization.

3. Ask each person to set goals for his or her own area of responsibility.

4. As a team, discuss each team member's goals and determine the degree of fit with the team goals and broader (short- and long-term) goals of the organization.

5. Resolve any differences between the individual and the team, as well as team and organizational goals.

6. Modify team and individual goals based on the discussion.

7. Discuss and establish methods for reaching goals.

8. Identify ways to measure achievement and establish timelines for monitoring progress.

9. Check for understanding of everyone's goals.

10. As a group, establish times when performance will be reviewed.

11. Write down every goal and review the list periodically.

Politics, Power, and Group Interaction

Leading and managing the process of change is imperative in today's group practice, and in many ways it is one of the most difficult tasks facing the medical practice executive. Today, governance is not about the maintenance of the medical practice or the casual oversight of management. It is about the intense efforts to transform medical practices into effective healthcare delivery models that will thrive into the future.

This requires governing bodies to be more than caretakers. They must also exert active leadership. The board must be more than a collection of advocates for a cause. It must be a mission-driven body of individuals who bring different perspectives and talents to the meeting, with the single purpose of advancing the mission of the group. The mission, goals, policies, procedures, and values of the organization have to be documented. In addition, every member of the organization should align behaviors to encourage adoption of these key success factors. This requires consistency, leadership, and, above all, hard work and perseverance.

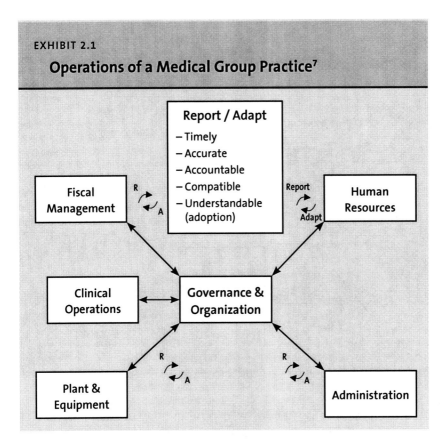

EXHIBIT 2.1

Operations of a Medical Group Practice[7]

All of this makes governance one of the most significant issues for the medical group practice today. What makes a group practice a focused and effective organization has much more to do with how the governance structure is organized than it does with the practice's legal structure. As Exhibits 2.1 and 2.2 illustrate, the interaction of governance and operational activities is essential for the effective execution of the group's mission and to ensure, through monitoring those activities, that it will further the organization's mission.

Medical groups are traditionally viewed as professional collegial organizations. They have many unique features. Some of the features that affect governance are that the primary producers are the owners (in many cases), the governed are also the governors (which leads to many policy quandaries), and the pervasive notion is that one's particular view should be considered above all else. This proprietorship mentality

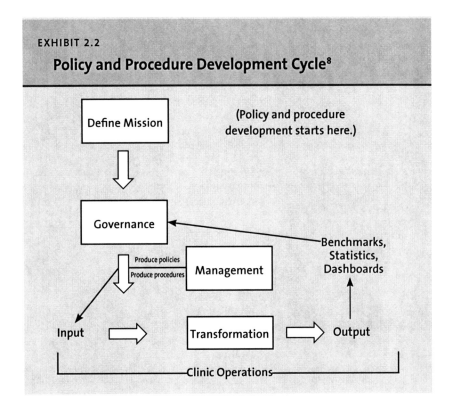

EXHIBIT 2.2

Policy and Procedure Development Cycle[8]

leads to numerous issues for the governing body of the practice. Not unlike the U.S. government system, at some point the need to have continuity in governance and the need for more nimble business actions outweighs the need for a strict "one-person, one-vote" rule or the consensus approach that characterizes many group practice organizations.

This issue becomes more difficult, as well as more important, as a group becomes larger and more diverse. Eventually, the need for a more centralized representational form of governance becomes important for many of the following reasons:

- It becomes more difficult for members of the group to find time to participate and to bring enough members of the group together to make policies and other decisions.

- Information disequilibrium increases. Some people are aware of and understand the issues, but some do not. This may be caused by poor communication or the lack of time to understand the issue or to become informed.

- The geographic limitations of attendance at meetings and other necessary absences from meetings make it difficult to address important issues.

- There is a general lack of interest in some topics needing discussion.

- The group members sense that they do not understand the issues or that their participation is not needed or welcomed.

Stephen Wagner states in "Defining the ACMPE Fellow," "You cannot continually provide energy to a cause that you cannot champion, to a vision you can't share, to an organization you cannot believe in."[9] Medical groups must require more of the participants in their governance structure and move beyond micromanagement to leadership and transform their way of thinking. Transformational leadership requires a group change in thinking, a change in vocabulary, and a shift of paradigms.

Medical practice executives must lead, not just manage. Management is focused on the maintenance of the status quo. Medical practice executives can change the organization by leading and by creating the understanding that the status quo may not be in the best interest of the group or the individual in the future. The role of the physician administrator team is to help the members of the medical group understand what the possibilities are; the role of leaders is to help them embrace a compelling vision of the future. Groups must move from an ad hoc method of policy development and decision making to a more systematic process that allows for the coordination of governance and management.

Implementing Change

Medical practice executives must address change in the practice with preparation and diligence. To affect change, the organization must have a compelling reason to change. There must be a vision of what they are trying to achieve, what success looks like, and why. Asking people to leave what they know for something unknown will not end well without a plan. The journey, no matter how long, includes uncertainty. Uncertainty can paralyze an organization.

The chances of success are improved by including the entire organization in planning the change. Members of the staff and the entire leadership team must be motivated and included in the planning process. By including staff members in planning for changes that will affect them, it will empower the team to help create its future, reduce anxiety, and improve the chance of success.

Change often fails because of failure to effectively communicate the vision, progress, and successes along the way. Communication — the two-way kind — is critical to this process. Share information through formal and informal channels and ensure it is timely, consistent, and transparent. Anxiety and uncertainty is reduced through clear, effective communications.

Leadership is responsible for setting the tone, knowing the way forward, and leading the way. Without an effective leadership team, no change initiative can succeed. While staff members want to believe, trust, and follow the leadership, change initiatives depend on it. The leadership team's failure to lead is often the cause of change failure.

Managing the day-to-day impacts of the change initiative is key. Planning is important, and execution is critical. Having a strong and effective management team to lead the process is a major contributing factor to change success, and lack thereof is also a major factor in change failure. The communication process employs management. The process of motivation and buy-in requires management, as does the process of visioning. Management is integral to the process, a leading factor that contributes to either success or failure.

Plans involving change must employ specific, measurable, achievable, realistic, and timely (*SMART*) goals. Execution is critical for change success and SMART goals are critical for effective execution. The more specific the goals, the greater the chance of success. Change occurs in small steps. The ability to plan milestones along the way, measure their achievement, celebrate their success, and have a goal for the next step all contribute to the success of change efforts.

Executing change initiative is not simple, but it is necessary in today's environment. Failure to change — as well as to adapt to changing conditions — can easily result in organizational stagnation and failure. Control what can be controlled, manage what can be managed, and communicate effectively.

::: Ethical Oversight

Today's medical practice environment is characterized by competition, a growing scarcity of resources, government encroachment, and increased consumer demands, all of which have created new ethical dilemmas for medical group practices. A number of issues common to most healthcare professions and organizations create ethical dilemmas, such as meeting the healthcare needs of the community, patients' rights, patient confidentiality, and indigent care. Some ethical issues and dilemmas are dissimilar enough from these common issues to warrant their separate review. The following issues presented in a question format illustrate possible ethical conflicts:

- **Payment and medical care and services**
  - Is there a difference in the quality or adequacy of care provided based on the method of payment?
  - Are specific medical services discouraged by the patient's inability to pay?
  - Are patients referred to a hospital emergency room because of the nature of the emergency, or because of the lack of adequate reimbursement from third-party payers?
  - In accordance with collection policies, are patients denied care because of their inability to pay at the time services are requested?
- **Fees and coding**
  - Are fees established based on the systematic cost and fee analysis or relative value units, or are they based on the level of third-party reimbursement?
  - Are fees for some services increased to make up for services not adequately reimbursed by third-party payers?
  - Is creative coding encouraged to establish a level of service that maximizes reimbursement, or does it accurately reflect the appropriate level of service for the presenting problem?
  - Are increased costs incurred by the medical group automatically transferred to the patient in the form of increased patient fees?

- **Promotion**
    - Are the costs of advertising justifiable, given the high price of healthcare delivery?
    - Is it appropriate to compare the quality of care among providers in public?

A practice executive's ethical principles evolve as a result of upbringing, experiences, spiritual convictions, and training. Ethical principles direct our commitments to a course of action and guide in making choices. Practice executives assume a responsibility to their community and to society in general. They have a higher obligation than the bottom line of a financial statement.

Today's practice administrators provide the managerial direction for the organization. They have the opportunity to direct the establishment of clear and concise ethical standards for their groups. Ethical decisions that confront medical practice organizations cannot be ignored. Clear standards and objectives are critical in guiding the medical group toward its stated goal while reflecting the values, commitment, and sensitivity of the organization and its personnel.

⠿ Group Dynamics and Group Culture

The subject of group culture will come up often in any discussion of group governance and organizational dynamics because culture (or the absence of culture) lies at the center of change and decision making. Simply stated, organizational culture is how things are done in an organization — its beliefs, patterns of behavior, shared values, and traditions. Culture is shaped by myriad sources.

For medical groups, some of those sources are:

- Professional training;
- Traditions of the group;
- The specialty and type of group;
- Policies and procedures;
- Communication style;

- How much documentation of methodology is done and accepted; and
- The personalities of the group members and staff.

Conclusion

Effective management of the practice's culture is no easy task, but it is the responsibility of the medical practice executive. A practice built on clear organizational structure, a shared vision, consistent communication, fair conflict resolution, and consistent decision-making processes will be successful in building a culture of trust and respect.

Notes

1. J.M. Kouzes and B.Z. Posner, *The Leadership Challenge* (San Francisco: Jossey-Bass, 2003), 87.
2. C.A. O'Reilly, "Corporations, Culture, and Commitment: Motivation and Social Control in Organizations," *California Management Review* 23 (1989): 9–17.
3. Edgar H. Schein, *Organizational Culture and Leadership* (San Francisco: Jossey-Bass, 1988).
4. Patrick Lencioni, *The Five Dysfunctions of a Team: A Leadership Fable* (San Francisco: Jossey-Bass, 2002): 195–221.
5. Ralph Stayer, "How I Learned to Let My Workers Lead," *Harvard Business Review* (November/December 1990): 66–88.
6. W.A. Schiemann, "Aligning People Achieve Top Performance" *Leadership Excellence*. (August 2007): 20.
7. © 2005 Jones and Bartlett Publishers, Inc. Reprinted with permission.
8. © 2005 Jones and Bartlett Publishers, Inc. Reprinted with permission.
9. Stephen L. Wagner, "Defining the ACMPE Fellow," *College View* (Fall 2003): 27–30.

Part II

Patient-Centered Care

::: Introduction

Managing the patient-centered care of the medical practice organization is an increasingly important portion of the practice administrator's job. From creating and monitoring patient workflow to promoting appropriate patient communication to developing, implementing, and maintaining standards of care, the successful administrator must become adept at the skills required. In addition to evaluating performance quality compared to industry benchmarks, the practice administrator is an important component of the organization's patient-centered care team. Chapters 3 and 4 follow the blueprint designed by practicing medical practice executives to describe the key competencies, knowledge, and skills required to develop and maintain effective patient-centered care in the medical practice.

The major areas of competence in patient-centered care, as identified by certified and fellow members of the Medical Group Management Association are to provide an environment to create, implement, and maintain care coordination processes that lead to the best patient outcomes and to design, implement, and maintain quality initiatives and measurement activities.

Within both chapters in Part II, these major competencies are further delineated according to the key knowledge and skills required to demonstrate competency as a manager of patient-centered care. A few examples of these supporting skills are creating and monitoring patient workflow, monitoring continuity of care and providing feedback, and implementing corrective action.

Chapter 3

Patient-Centered Care: An Overview

When looking at patient-centered care from a broad perspective, it is clear that this domain is in a state of change as it attempts to maintain balance while also changing to meet the demands and expectations of the individual stakeholders as well as society as a whole. The medical practice administrator should take the time to identify and understand the specific pressures of operations as well as core issues within other domains that also affect this area.

The overarching framework of the Institute for Healthcare Improvement's Triple Aim centers on patient-centered care. Three dimensions of this framework are improving the patient experience, including quality and satisfaction; reducing the costs of healthcare; and improving health outcomes. As a medical practice administrator, your first area of attention and an area to involve your staff members in should be improving the patient experience. Patient-centered care should be the focus of every practice.

An important part of patient-centered care is looking at space design and patient flow with efficiency and patient satisfaction in mind. It is a method of determining a unique set of best practice standards established by key personnel and team members who are mindful of cultural differences and population management challenges. The resulting standards become incorporated into every organizational change, whether it is architectural design, space planning, or staff interaction.

⠿ Creating and Monitoring Workflow

For a practice to be efficient and allow the physician and staff to focus on patient care, attention should be paid to how patients and tasks flow within the organization. This flow, from a patient's perspective, includes the four primary steps of:

1. Making an appointment;

2. Entering the office;

3. Receiving treatment from the physician; and

4. Leaving the office satisfied that you received high-quality healthcare.

Although patients do not see the behind-the-scenes workflows, they are affected by any breakdowns that occur within these flows. A significant portion of patient satisfaction with the practice is determined by the efficiency, accuracy, and effectiveness of the steps that are accomplished behind the scenes. Analysis of patient flow should be undertaken, including the posting of charges and payments, filing of medical records, and processing of medical record copy requests. Examples of this type of analysis as applied to the first stage of the patient-centered and business workflows are shown in Exhibits 3.1 and 3.2.[1]

Patient Workflow

Issues that may upset or aggravate patients during the patient workflow cycle include extensive delays in the waiting room, not being advised to bring specific documents with them to the appointment with the physician, extended waiting times in the examination room, and the inability to get timely follow-up appointments when leaving the offices of the practice.

Clinical flow begins long before the patient arrives in the practice's offices. Examination rooms need to be stocked, preferably in a standardized manner, with the supplies that may be required by the physician or staff. By standardizing both the items to be stored in each examination room and their locations within each examination room, staff members will be able to reduce the amount of time needed to search for a specific everyday item. An alternative to maintaining stocks of supplies within each examination room is the use of small supply rooms or cabinets

EXHIBIT 3.1

Typical Patient Flow Process at Check-In

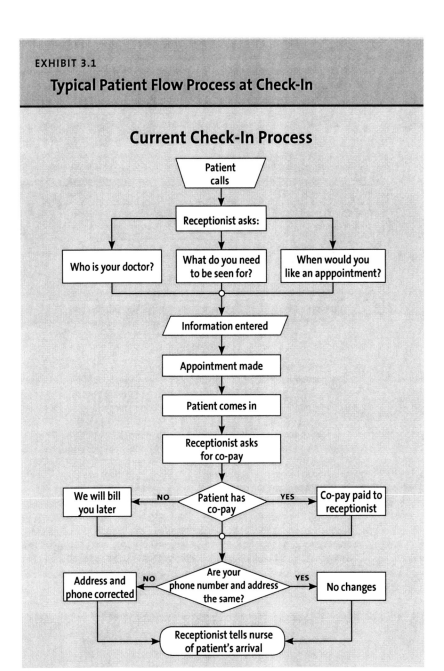

Current Check-In Process

Patient calls

Receptionist asks:

Who is your doctor? | What do you need to be seen for? | When would you like an apppointment?

Information entered

Appointment made

Patient comes in

Receptionist asks for co-pay

We will bill you later ← NO — Patient has co-pay — YES → Co-pay paid to receptionist

Address and phone corrected ← NO — Are your phone number and address the same? — YES → No changes

Receptionist tells nurse of patient's arrival

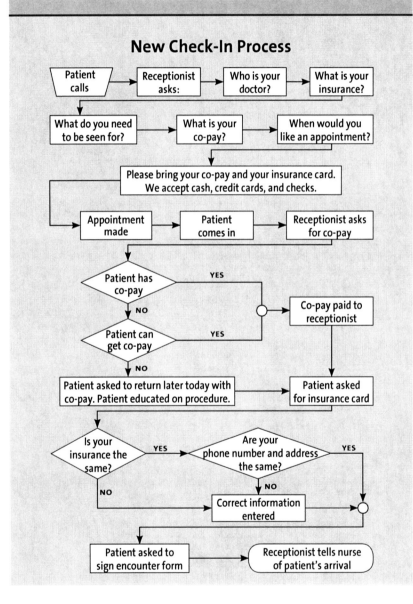

EXHIBIT 3.2

Efficient Patient Flow Process at Check-In

New Check-In Process

close to several examination rooms. Although potentially increasing the walking required of the clinical support staff, this method of maintaining supply stocks will reduce the overall amount of supplies that need to be maintained in inventory.

Medical records need to be reviewed before the patient's arrival to ensure that all test results are available and that any required instruments or testing materials are available for the physician's use. Preplanning each visit and ensuring that the required information and supplies are available can reduce the amount of time needed for each visit, enabling physicians to be more efficient.

Breakdown of a Patient Visit

On arrival, the patient begins the direct, on-site involvement by checking in at the practice's reception desk. At that time, the patient is identified and greeted by the reception staff. A new patient is normally asked to complete various intake documents, providing the demographic and billing and insurance information, whereas an established patient will normally be asked to review and confirm the information on file. The patient may then be asked to provide copayment and any referral documents that may be appropriate. After completion of the required paperwork, a member of the clinical support staff normally escorts the patient to an examination room.

In addition to the direct hands-on care provided by both the physician and the clinical staff for the patient, there are several other areas within the clinical encounter that may require action by the physician or staff. These tasks, based on the needs of the patient, may include:

- Developing and documenting a treatment plan that addresses the patient's medical needs;

- Providing needed educational support to the patient, which may include reviewing a videotape or providing printed material on the issues that concern the patient;

- Ensuring that the patient has provided informed consent for procedures that are being scheduled; and

- Initiating any referrals or other carrier-required documents that may be needed by the patient to obtain the care indicated in the plan of treatment.

After providing the services that are required by the patient, the remainder of the clinical workflow for the staff consists of escorting the patient from the examination area and cleaning and preparing the examination room for the next patient. For the patient, the final step is checkout, where the patient receives the required documents and forms, makes any future appointments with the practice, and pays for any costs that may be due and were not collected at time of check-in. For the physician, the final part of the clinical workflow process is made up of properly documenting the patient history, the clinical services provided, and the plan for future services. Determining the procedure and diagnostic codes to be used to categorize this patient's visit is usually the last step in this process for the physician.

Patient Flow Patterns

A smooth operational flow on office visits from check-in to checkout creates a better experience for the patient. Efficient patient flow is the only way to maximize the practice's most important asset — the physician's time. It is the fundamental service–revenue equation:

Physician Provides Patient Care → Patient Care Generates Revenue

Patient flow encompasses all the steps in the patient care sequence. It involves telephone usage, appropriate scheduling, efficient registration and check-in, satisfactory waiting experience, effective patient care in the examination room, and smooth checkout.

Physicians will focus on the clinical highlight of the patient flow sequence, which is the actual physician–patient encounter. However, it's important for the practice manager to understand all the parts of patient flow. Preparation and follow-up by staff ensure that the examination encounter goes smoothly.

The next sections will spotlight key operational elements within the patient flow including:

- Telephone usage and protocols;
- Triage systems;
- Call coverage;
- Patient scheduling;
- Registration, check-in, and waiting; and
- Checkout.

Telephone Usage

Effective practice managers know that communications are critical to good patient care and that the telephone plays a key part in this vital function. Effective use of the telephone for scheduling, referrals, patient triage, answering patient questions, ordering and renewing prescriptions, handling insurance claims, and ordering supplies is mandatory for an efficient practice. Today, the phone is often just a part of a telecommunications system that includes use of the Internet and e-mail for many of these tasks. However, the phone continues to play a major part in practice communications.

All of these options can increase practice efficiency. For example, automated attendants, which answer and route calls after prompting the patient, are now standard in many practices. An automated attendant does the work of a full-time-equivalent employee by routing calls to the appropriate source without human intervention. Typically, no more than five options are offered because more can frustrate callers. Such options include:

- Scheduling an appointment;
- Speaking with a triage nurse;
- Discussing a bill;
- Refilling a prescription; and
- Speaking with an operator.

Telephone Protocols

Telephone protocols are typically used to help staff members make and answer low-urgency calls without consulting a physician. Such protocols include:

- Answering all calls within a standard number of rings (e.g., two) and repeating a standard greeting using provided scripting;
- Accepting and handling appointment calls courteously;
- Handling emergency calls calmly and quickly;
- Directing calls from hospitals and physicians appropriately; and
- Responding to routine billing questions competently.

Triage Systems

In a medical practice, triage — prioritizing medical treatment based on urgency — is typically done by a triage nurse who handles patient calls related to questions or concerns. Many of the questions a patient typically asks can be answered by the nurse following specific protocols.

Triage systems can increase patient satisfaction and help the physicians to better manage their time. Typical triage systems include:

- Physician-approved guidelines for treatment;
- Procedures for documentation;
- Appropriate responses to calls about emergent, urgent, and nonurgent problems; and
- Guidelines for categorizing calls as life-threatening, urgent, important, and routine, and appropriate response times.

Written guidelines serve as training and procedural documents along with physician authorizations for releasing certain information. Triage calls are handled according to callers' symptoms and/or needs; appropriate protocols are specialty and symptom specific.

Every clinical phone call to the practice should be documented in a standard manner within the patient chart. Most documentation is done electronically. This allows for the information and messages to be transmitted from the nurse to the physician and back seamlessly. Documentation of all telephone calls and advice given must be placed in patients' medical records.

Appropriate education and training of staff members performing the triage function is essential. Triage staff members must be qualified and able to assess a problem, provide information, and know when to refer the problem to the physician. The practice administrator must be comfortable with their judgment because ultimately the practice is liable for the advice given. Nurses perform most triage functions because they have the necessary skill level and licensure to evaluate medical problems.

Call Coverage

Often, physicians may be responsible for their own call coverage from 7 a.m. on Monday morning until 5 p.m. on Friday afternoon. Typical call coverage includes:

- After-hours emergencies;
- Patient questions; and
- Hospital rounds.

Call coverage for a group practice often depends on how many hospitals the practice covers, the trauma designation of the hospital and required call response times, and how many physicians or providers within the practice share the call coverage. Small group practices usually designate one physician to take call, with a second doctor identified as backup. In a larger practice, more physicians must be available to cover the larger patient base.

With hospital call, the medical staff bylaws at each hospital the practice is affiliated with must be checked to determine how often the physicians are expected to be on call for unassigned emergency room duty.

Handling the communications among the physicians when on call needs to be clearly communicated among the group's answering service, other physicians, and patients. Do physicians prefer text messages or phone calls? Do adjustments need to be made during certain hours? Is there a contingency plan in place if a doctor cannot be reached?

An answering service experienced in helping medical practices is often used to receive off-hours calls and route them to the appropriate after-hours on-call physician. The protocol typically includes having the primary incoming telephone line placed on call forwarding to the answering service each weekday evening and on Fridays for the weekend (unless weekend hours are offered). This will ensure that all patients, the emergency room, and the hospital have immediate access to the physician on call.

Patient Scheduling

The framework for patient activity within the practice is determined by the day's schedule of appointments. "Good scheduling demands good planning, good data, good information systems, and, above all, good staff; that is, workers who are trained, committed, and empowered to provide top-notch customer service."[2]

To properly develop an appointment schedule that allows the provider to be efficient and to anticipate staffing needs, the development of patient demand projections needs to occur. These projections are based on several factors, including patient demand variations, and should be conducted based on the day of the week and time of day; age of patients, which can affect the amount of time needed for the provider–patient interaction; and the specialty and personality of the physician, which can also affect the amount of time needed for the provider–patient interaction.

Other factors that can affect a daily schedule, but cannot be as easily projected, include emergencies; calls from hospitals, nursing homes, and other physicians; and last-minute cancellations and no-shows. Some of these issues can be anticipated, and schedule modifications and office procedures can be implemented in an effort to reduce their negative effects.

Many scheduling methodologies can be used to alleviate some of these variations. There are three general methods of scheduling:

1. **Single intervals.** Each visit receives the same amount of time (e.g., 15 minutes) on the scheduling calendar, regardless of the type of visit or patient complaint.

2. **Multiple intervals.** The intervals between appointments (e.g., 15–30 minutes) depend on the type of visit (e.g., new) or the patient complaint (e.g., health check).

3. **Block intervals.** A single block of time (e.g., on the hour and half hour) is established for multiple appointments regardless of the visit type or patient complaint. Scheduling several patients to arrive at the same time decreases any downtime for the physician because there are always patients available to be seen. This increases patient wait times, as some patients must wait from the time they arrive until the other patients in that time block are seen.

Most practices use multiple intervals because it allows them to estimate the amount of time a patient may need and to balance this with patient waiting time.

Other approaches include the following:

- **Individual scheduling**, which provides a time slot for each patient. A no-show or late arrival affects the entire schedule. The physician loses time if the patient has to be rescheduled.

- **Modified wave scheduling,** which clusters patients at the beginning of each hour or block of time, followed by individual appointments every 10, 15, or 20 minutes during the rest of the hour or block. Specific types of appointments can be scheduled at certain time periods depending on the length of time of those appointments. For example, two sick-patient appointments would follow one for a physical exam. The medical assistant can room one patient while the physician sees another. This distributes patient flow evenly through the physician's day and decreases patient wait time.

- **Open access scheduling,** which is built on having open slots when the day begins so that a patient can be seen the same day as he or she calls. If the patient requests an appointment on another day, the patient is scheduled accordingly. Depending on the medical specialty, 30 to 50 percent of the appointments remain open for same-day calls. Open-access scheduling allows today's work to be done today. It also increases patient satisfaction because patients can be seen the same day they call for an appointment.

As every new practice manager soon learns, scheduling is a complex and challenging task. Practices will experience patients who do not appear for the appointment (no-shows), patients who are habitually or occasionally late, and patients or staff members with emergencies. Plans and protocols must anticipate such situations so there is the least impact possible to patient flow. To reduce the risk of no-shows, staff members can be assigned or computer systems implemented to call patients to remind them of their appointments; appointment slots can be held open to allow for last-minute add-ons; and the judicious use of double-booking can be implemented to compensate for last-minute cancellations and no-shows.

One scheduling challenge occasionally arises, which is how to deal appropriately with disabled individuals. Physicians cannot refuse to treat patients because of their disabilities. For example, a practice cannot refuse to treat a patient with HIV or AIDS, conditions protected under the Americans with Disabilities Act of 1990 (ADA). Similarly, a physician's practice can't refuse to treat a person with a hearing impairment because it can't or doesn't want to pay for interpreter services.

The ADA mandates that a medical organization must provide, at its expense, auxiliary aids such as qualified interpreters, Braille materials, and large-print materials. More expensive auxiliary aids may not be required if they create an "undue burden." The ADA makes allowances for an undue burden that results in "significant difficulty or expense." What constitutes undue burden for a small practice vs. a large practice will differ. Undue burden is determined on a case-by-case basis.

Registration Process and Patient Check-In

When the patient arrives for an appointment, the registration process is an important part of how that person views a practice.

The check-in experience begins the moment the patient opens the door. Put yourself in the position of the patient. What do you see? The reception area or waiting room space forms one of the first impressions the patient has of the practice. The area should present an updated, well-lit décor and have adequate and comfortable seating. An outdated, dirty, cluttered waiting room gives a negative impression of the entire practice. Even magazines several months old can convey an outdated image.

The reception area is also one place to ensure that there are no office design barriers for people with disabilities. Architectural barrier regulations address many physical aspects that allow accommodation of those with disabilities, such as handicap-accessible restrooms, access to the building (e.g., ramps to navigate stairs, elevators, and automated doors), and parking set aside for the disabled. Any new construction or renovations must meet ADA standards. Practice managers should regularly review their office space to ensure that it offers easy access for people with disabilities.

Reception staff members should be able to see and monitor the waiting areas so they can help any patient with special needs. A patient may become ill or anxious while waiting, so a clear view of these areas is critical. Patients will become upset if they have to wait longer than they think they should, so consider posting a sign stating your waiting time goal — usually no more than 20 minutes — to help set patient expectations. If the schedule gets off track (e.g., a physician was delayed at the hospital or a patient took extra time), the receptionist can communicate that fact to patients.

Particular attention should be paid to how the reception area is designed to ensure patient confidentiality. The Health Insurance Portability and Accountability Act of 1996 makes compliance of paramount importance and this must be considered in office design. The reception area is often a place where inadvertent breaches of confidentiality can occur. Two staff members may be discussing a patient and not notice that others in the area can overhear. Hallways, restrooms, and clinical areas are also areas where confidentiality is sometimes forgotten.

In a busy practice, the receptionist may forget to look up when a patient enters and, as a result, the patient feels invisible and unwelcome. This lack of greeting may be a sign of an inappropriately staffed front desk and should be corrected. The role of receptionist is similar to that of a juggler. Not only do these staff members set the scene and the mood for the incoming patient, they also have many tasks to complete quickly and accurately. They must:

- Ensure that the reception area stays attractive and comfortable;
- Greet each patient with enthusiasm and respect;
- Pay attention to patients during the registration process so they feel welcome and not like they're interrupting;
- Protect the patient's privacy with appropriate confidentiality procedures (e.g., sign-in methods);
- Be sensitive to the practice's waiting-time goal (e.g., 20 minutes) and inform patients of the reason for any delays;
- Collect accurate, up-to-date clinical and billing information; and
- Collect any funds due, such as copayments, deductibles, and past balances.

Exhibit 3.3 is a checklist for reviewing the accuracy of the patient registration process.

Checkout

The patient's visit is not finished after the provider completes the exam or other service. It is up to the physician and/or practice employees to ensure that the patient understands any follow-up steps that must be taken, such as an X-ray or a laboratory test. If additional services or a referral are recommended, the patient must understand what is

EXHIBIT 3.3

Reviewing Accuracy of Patient Registration Process

	Yes	No
Does the staff accurately gather patient information including: ■ Name, address, phone number, and Social Security number; ■ Employment information; ■ Guarantor information; and ■ Insurance information, including copayment and expiration date?		
Are appropriate forms signed and dated, including: ■ Financial guarantee; ■ Authorization to treat; and ■ Other required forms?		

required to obtain a preauthorization or a referral from the payer and who will complete those steps. The patient must understand what the insurer will cover and what they will be expected to pay for additional services. The practice must also obtain payment from the patient to cover the copayment or other charges incurred that day, if this was not done during check-in.

Exhibit 3.4 is a checklist for completing the patient's checkout process.

::: Patient Communication and Patient Engagement

Good communication is critical to good patient care and to patient flow. Most times, an initial telephone call, often for an urgent need, sets the tone for a new patient's first impression of the practice. A smooth operational flow on each visit helps create a good experience for patients and increases the chances that they will return.

EXHIBIT 3.4

Completion of Patient Checkout Process

	Yes	No
Does the patient understand preauthorization or referral request processes?		
Are copayments collected at registration or at the end of the appointment?		
Does the staff discuss the payment options that are available to the patient (credit cards, cash, checks)?		

Many of these outcomes can be avoided by simple patient communication. When confirming appointments, practices should remind patients of the documents and forms that they should bring to their appointments. Many of these forms are unique to specific insurance carriers (e.g., Medicare, Medicaid, employer plans, and commercial carriers) and plans, and may include referrals and procedure precertifications. Communicating with the patient, explaining what is going on, and reassuring him or her can usually mitigate any annoyance or aggravation on the patient's part. Sufficient time should also be included within each visit to allow the physician to dictate notes and to respond to issues that become known during the visit with the patient.

Patients are key stakeholders in any medical practice, and you must do everything possible to keep them informed and actively involved in their healthcare outcomes. This includes communicating with them in a variety of ways, including traditional methods, such as telephone calls and letters, to more modern systems, such as Websites and patient portals.

Patient Communication Protocols

Verbal communication is the primary method used to convey health information to patients about their diagnosis and treatment options; however, verbal communication is fraught with difficulty. Supplementing verbal communication with written information and instruction is an essential part of establishing effective patient communication protocols. Written material affords a patient the opportunity to read and reflect on information when opportune, not just when he or she consults with the physician. Written brochures are usually readily available from professional associations as well as online.[3]

Medical practice executives should clearly outline patient communication protocols so that all patients will receive the information necessary to make informed treatment decisions. Protocols should establish step-by-step instructions and include methods to assess patient understanding of physician instructions. Use of effective communication protocols will ensure that patients are informed; thus such procedures can also be an effective risk management strategy.

Often, a patient's experience is linked to engagement, and we know that involving patients and caregivers in care plans leads to improved outcomes and patient satisfaction. Incorporating the patient's lifestyle, habits, literacy, comprehension, and support system into the treatment plans will also increase the chances of successful intervention and compliance.

Sometimes creating ways to enhance patient access to medical care can be as simple as offering more flexible office hours or implementing more efficient communication. Patient portals, e-mail, videoconferencing, or an interactive Website will offer patients a variety of channels to exchange information.

Staffing and Roles

It might be necessary to add staff members to effectively and efficiently manage patient communication needs. As insurance premiums and deductibles increase, patients are financially responsible for high proportions of their healthcare expenses. At the time of service, they are expected to pay for their portion with health savings accounts, flexible savings accounts, or out of pocket. Patients who are new to health insurance coverage, networks, or plans might need assistance from practice staff before their visits to understand how their insurance works and what it covers.

Staff members can investigate a patient's plan to see how much is left to pay on a deductible and what portion of coinsurance the patient is responsible for paying. By connecting electronically with payers to access real-time adjudication, eligibility, and verification of benefit status, staff members can help a patient understand his or her financial responsibility, coverage and benefits, and anticipate the payment obligation.

Practices can also create payment policies and fee schedules. The patient experience can be improved by providing multiple payment methods, offering options for third-party financing, and using easy-to-read statements. Practices should consider having multiple registration staff members or implementing kiosks for check-in as well as having a patient portal for online payments and billing communication.

Another way practices assist with the changing patient needs is by incorporating other new staff members or adjusting staffing roles to create positions such as care managers to help identify high-risk patients, care gaps, and compliance barriers. These staff members can be hired specifically for care coordination and case management or to serve in dual roles as clinicians or office staff in combination with other duties.

Depending on their training and experience, these professionals help ensure that patients understand how to implement a physician's instructions. In some practices, through behavioral interviews and motivational coaching, staff members can be instrumental in identifying patients who have complex needs or are at higher-than-average risk for complications and compliance because of socioeconomic conditions, lack of support systems, or limited literacy and comprehension. These trained professionals can also implement maintenance and preventive surveillance with early intervention and increased observation. Wellness programs, including lifestyle discussions, peer interactions, and group visits can also be implemented to address a patient's needs.

As administrators look at the bigger picture of patient care and population health, their focus is shifting away from an emphasis on operational aspects into more clinical facets. Using systems to evaluate and manage care for groups of patients broadens the scope of observation and the actions that will be required.

Administrators are also working more closely with clinical staff members to manage teamwork and group dynamics in their practices. Operating efficiently and effectively might involve team care plan oversight and daily huddles to discuss incoming patients. Monitoring trends by patient, diagnosis, and population requires a high level of vigilance and engagement from the administrator, clinicians, and staff members.

Communication Systems

The needs, limitations, and requirements of those who use a particular communication system (e.g., voice mail, e-mail, and electronic health record [EHR] system) should be the first consideration when designing and implementing communication processes. These requirements include defining the goals, expectations, and capabilities of the users of the communication system, including physicians, staff members, patients, vendors, and any other stakeholder group that may require access to the practice.

The sophistication of the communication system is often dependent on the level of sophistication of the users. If some users, such as elderly patients, are not computer literate, it is important to provide multiple avenues for communication to ensure that these patients can access the services provided by the practice.

The primary goal of patients is to have access to a communication system that allows them to communicate with the physician and the support staff as appropriate. Patients need to be able to make and change appointments, ask questions, obtain prescription renewals and referrals, request records, and discuss myriad other issues that are extremely important to the patient. Physicians and practice staff want a system by which they can communicate among themselves and with other healthcare providers and organizations, respond to patient requests, and attend to the normal business activities of the practice — and to do it all in an efficient and cost-effective manner.

Telephones and Voice Mail

The most obvious methods of communication include telephone, voice mail, fax, Internet, e-mail, pagers, and point-to-point delivery as serviced by the U.S. Postal Service, FedEx, UPS, and others. Each form of communication has its own purpose, which is normally derived from its individual strengths and weaknesses.

The most obvious and prevalent communication tool in use in practices is the telephone. Along with often being the first point of communication with patients, the telephone can act as a marketing tool, providing information about the practice through a message-on-hold program. This message does need to be updated on a regular basis, such as every three to six months, to keep it from becoming stale and outdated. After normal office hours, the telephone can be forwarded to any number of answering services who can augment the physician's office by taking and forwarding the appropriate messages and calls to the on-call physician, thereby ensuring a patient's 24-hour access to medical support.

While telephone systems are a necessary support for any medical practice, they may also create challenges. Frustration among all of the users of the system will occur when a telephone system is not designed properly, resulting in calls that are not routed to the appropriate staff member, or when there are not enough lines to respond to the demand for access. Even where there are sufficient lines, the lack of an adequate number of properly trained staff members to answer and respond to the volume of calls will also cause significant issues. Many users of telephone systems are intolerant of voice mail systems and are frustrated when calls are not returned on a timely basis. To reduce complaints concerning the use of voice mail systems, a practice needs to develop and implement detailed guidelines concerning expectations with regard to clearing and responding to voice mail messages. The use of auto-attendant and voice mail systems can become extremely confusing, especially for the elderly patient.

Proper, detailed planning is the best route to avoid or mitigate many of the weaknesses of a telephone system. This planning may include:

- Exploring the use of call centers to receive and direct calls;
- Defining call flow, including the use of hunt groups (a series of telephone lines identified as a group such that if one line is busy, the next available line is used — it *hunts* for the next line) and triage systems for handling inbound calls;
- Developing answering standards; and
- Identifying emergency call protocols.

Patient Portals and Online Information

Most practices today use many facets of the Internet to communicate. A practice's Website is one vehicle that is used to make information available to potential and current patients, referring physicians, and the community at large. A properly designed and easy-to-navigate Website also has the capability of reducing the volume of telephone calls received by a practice by enabling patients to refill pharmaceuticals, request chart copies, download forms, obtain directions, and ask questions via a patient portal.

Patient portals are a newer and near-universal tool that practices use to give patients better access to and control over all of their medical information. Features vary, but the basics include giving patients the ability to check a complete history of lab test results, interactively schedule appointments, and securely communicate with their healthcare team (including uploading and downloading files and accessing personalized patient education materials).

In addition to providing practice-specific information, Websites and patient portals can provide medical education as well as links to other Websites concerning medical conditions and procedures that would otherwise result in telephone calls or extended office visits. Through the use of interactive programs located on a practice's Website, patients can become educated on detailed matters such as surgical procedures being considered and the different types of clinical tests that the patient may receive.

This form of communication can be accomplished at the patient's convenience, with respect to both time and location. To be most effective, the practice Website and patient portal should contain current, accurate information and be easy for the user to navigate (see Exhibit 3.5 for an example).

Leveraging Technology

The Internet and other advances in technology have enabled even the smallest medical practices to engage in the practice of telehealth. Telehealth and telemedicine use technology to provide clinical and medical services over geographic distances, rather than by traditional face-to-face methods, in a timely and convenient manner. In addition, telehealth uses technology to deliver nonclinical medical services, such as patient education and administrative functions.[4]

Telehealth typically employs the use of interactive video to treat and interact with patients. Other telehealth methods include online discussion forums for the purpose of consultations and the ongoing management of patients. Telehealth can also provide patients and clinical professionals with education and training opportunities.

Staff Training

The medical practice is responsible for ensuring that all staff members and physicians receive sufficient training to become proficient and

EXHIBIT 3.5

EXHIBIT 3.5

Example of Using a Website to Educate Patients[5]

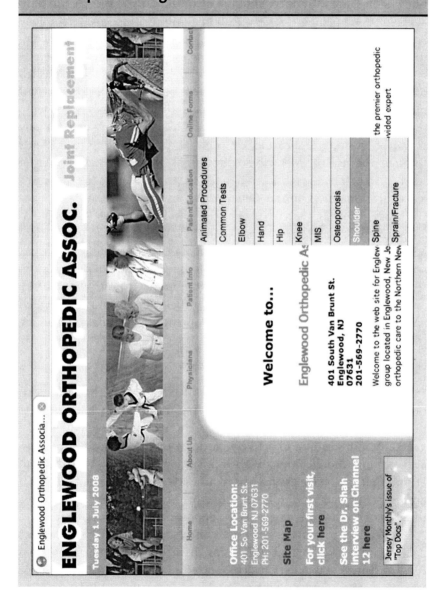

comfortable in the use of all of the software and technological tools that assist them in the performance of their duties. As new technologies (e.g., EHR systems, intra-office e-mail, and automated patient notification systems) are introduced into the medical practice, the need to train affected personnel increases. Some of the training in specific technology applications may require formal training sessions, whereas other modalities, such as reading manuals and online training, may also be used.

Even after initial training takes place, policies should be established to ensure that periodic refresher training is provided so individual staff members remain proficient and up to date on the specifics of the technology tools they are using. As mentioned, the Internet is an extremely powerful avenue to provide educational opportunities to patients through the use of interactive educational programs that can either reside on a practice's Website or be accessed through links to other medical educational sites on the Web.

Most physicians carry personal cell phones to enable the office or answering service to reach them when they are not in the office. These allow for two-way communication that was not possible with pagers, and smartphones can be an important tool for looking up information, sending e-mails, and taking voice calls from a single device. Just be aware that the phones physicians use for their practice must be secured and encrypted to avoid sharing private patient information if the phone is lost or stolen.

Patient Education

Patient education is a key component of patient-centered care. With proper education, patients can save money, understand what questions to ask, and improve their medical outcomes. Well-informed patients are generally more willing to actively participate in their healthcare management and more compliant with physician directives. Your job is to ensure that they have easy access to accurate, up-to-date materials that are simple to understand. An effective medical practice will institute a number of collaborative systems to support patient health literacy.

Educating patients is an important part of a medical practice's community outreach that also helps in maintaining practice visibility. Brochures, newsletters, videos, social media, and medical practice Websites are common delivery methods for patient education. The quality and content of these materials must be considered to ensure that the practice's aims and positioning goals are accomplished. In addition, because of the advances of technology and communication, there is a wider range of media a medical practice can take advantage of to reach patients.

⠿ Implementing Standards of Care

When focusing on providing patient-centered care and looking at improving patient experiences, improving health outcomes, and reducing healthcare costs, a practice needs to have standards of care developed, implanted, and tracked. Several potential standards of care were previously discussed including customer service centered on telephones, patient check-in, and patient flow. It is up to each practice to determine what the standard level of care for each service is. Once this is done, maintaining these standards is important.

Implementation of standards of care requires changes in both how the practice operates and how clinicians practice medicine. It is likely that the practice will need to redesign care processes to foster more staff coordination, including collaboration between the front office and providers to plug potential gaps in care. For example, the front office staff may need to contact patients and schedule appointments or tests proactively instead of waiting for the patients to call. But if the office staff doesn't know that the patient needs a specific test or if the physician fails to record the test in a patient's medical record, the visit is moot because the measure will not be met for that particular patient. Increased collaboration is needed to keep the front desk and the doctors on the same page. The whole staff has a role in meeting the standards.

Clinical Pathways

Clinical pathways are multidisciplinary plans of treatment that are developed to enable the implementation of clinical guidelines and protocols. While best known as *clinical pathways*, several other terms are used to describe this concept, including *care maps, integrated care pathways*, and *collaborative care pathways*.

Clinical pathways are used to support clinical, resource, and financial management of a patient with a specific condition over a specified time period. The four major components of the clinical pathway include (1) a timeline, (2) the type of care, (3) the outcome criteria, and

(4) the variance record for identifying deviations from the norms and/ or expectations.[6]

The goal of developing and implementing clinical pathways and clinical protocols is to attain a high level of quality medical care by identifying, implementing, and adhering to specific medical standards by all physicians in a given specialty when treating a specific set of symptoms or identified illness or injury. Through the application of clinical pathways in the utilization of clinical protocols, a group practice will have the tools to generate clinical data that will enable the organization to prove to outside entities the level of clinical quality being provided by the practice.

Clinical pathways and protocols can be derived from multiple sources, including third-party payers, medical specialty societies, and the National Institutes of Health. Even though applying these protocols constitutes good clinical care on its own, using audits and external assessments to measure compliance with the protocols can be used to confirm the quality of care being provided. This helps the practice negotiate better contracts with third-party payers and leads to improved relationships with local employers where direct contracting for medical services may be possible.

The effective development and implementation of clinical pathways within an organization requires a multidisciplinary approach, with input from all levels of clinical providers as well as input from nonclinical staff. The initial creation of this type of structure requires the full and unreserved endorsement and support of physicians as well as clinical and executive leadership of the organization. Preliminary meetings and discussions need to be held within the leadership structure to identify the organization-specific goals for the implementation of clinical pathways. In some cases, this may require the inclusion of various community collaborators who have involvement or responsibility for part of the care and treatment plan of the patient. Examples of this outside collaboration include visiting-nurse services, rehabilitation facilities, and social services support agencies.

In addition to being part of the leadership team, administrators can become advocates and facilitators, showing that the organization supports the implementation of clinical pathways. This is accomplished through words and by approving the necessary financial and operational resources to support the initiative.

In addition, the development and implementation of clinical pathways may have significant effects that go beyond the simple goal of quality care. The development and application of clinical pathway structures, when properly communicated to staff, patients, and community stakeholders, send a clear and effective message that the practice is committed to maintaining high-quality services. It also demonstrates effectiveness at both identifying and measuring the norms for improved patient care. Properly designed and implemented clinical pathways can also reduce the cost of care through changes in the services that will be rendered based on specific presented symptoms, and may have significant effect on insurance carrier–directed pay-for-performance models. The application of clinical pathways should also increase financial accountability through the elimination of redundancy and variations of clinical methods used by different providers.

Standards of care lead to improved satisfaction and improved quality outcomes for the individual patient and the population as a whole. Continuity of care is another standard that a practice should focus on, especially when adopting elements of population health.

::: Continuity of Care and Population Health

Continuity of Care

A perennial problem with continuity of care is that no matter how efficient your practice is or how good your staff is, noncompliant patients can undermine all of your efforts. Patient no-shows for appointments are a prime example, as they eat into your bottom line and trigger several negative chain reactions, including patients failing to rebook (making chronic problems tougher to manage) and scheduling problems caused by overbooking appointment slots to offset the no-shows.

One key aspect of continuity of care is making patients more accountable for ownership of their appointments, but many strategies in this regard either fail or are not enough on their own to make patients take charge. Techniques that are often helpful include securing appointments within 14 days of a new patient's requested time frame, reminder letters sent a week in advance of the appointment, automated phone calls made a week in advance (with an option to cancel by pressing a button), and personal phone calls made the day before the appointment and the day of the appointment.

Some practices are combining these techniques with another effective tactic of charging patients a $50 fee for each missed appointment. Medicaid patients are exempted by law, but by charging patients directly instead of going through their insurance company, no-show rates can be reduced dramatically.

Population Health

In population health there is a shift from a production-oriented system (e.g., standard treatments for acute illnesses, number of repeatable procedures per hour) to a focus on health risks and behaviors. In conventional healthcare delivery, technology often drives changes in acute and episodic care. Within population health management, behaviors, which are influenced by social networks, media, and clinicians, become the predominant force affecting health status, future costs, and health outcomes.

Because significant variation exists among different populations and within identified risk factors for those populations, standardized, repeatable interventions are difficult to develop. For example, while individuals at risk for lung cancer caused by smoking may be exposed to the same information, education, and counseling, behavior changes may occur as a result of family or personal experiences. In other words, small changes, such as a discussion with a trusted friend, may have far more impact than a well-designed, scalable health management and consumer education program.

Success in mitigating, controlling, or improving health risks requires multiple environments, including medical providers, work environments, families, social networks, and communities.

Elements for Population Health Management

A variety of models, ownership, and structures for population health management can achieve cost and quality outcomes depending on local customer needs, market circumstances, and organizational capabilities. With complex adaptive systems it may be more important for accountable care organizations (ACOs) to invest resources in understanding a population and identifying underlying health risks rather than focusing on specific models.

To ensure sustainability, funding for core processes needs to be shared. Health utilities, which can dramatically increase utilization and lower costs for critical support services, can be public–private partnerships that create, sponsor, and maintain community-based and shared resources used by clinical practices, consumers, health plans, and employers.

This model emphasizes an integrated set of core processes across a continuum of care. Some of the processes are provided by the clinical delivery system and others are provided by community stakeholders under the direction of clinicians.

Equally important is the array of processes that provide data, financial rewards for outcomes, tools to achieve improved performance, and a deliberate, focused change management strategy.

It is illogical to expect healthcare providers to make changes that produce diminished business results under the current fee-for-service payment system without an opportunity for financial incentives for improved outcomes. Payment reform from health plans and employers will take a variety of forms:

- Enhanced fee-for-service, such as grants, pay for performance, shared savings;

- Care management fees, such as direct payments for essential care coordination functions; or

- Global budgets, such as combining practitioner and facility payments for a bundle of services or all services for a patient or population.

Clinicians need a variety of tools that are integrated into and support clinical processes, but some experts say tools are more effective when they are shared by all clinicians treating a patient. Examples include an electronic prescribing system, clinical data registry, high-engagement electronic push messaging system, or patient call centers or outreach systems.

Continued experimentation, evaluation, and refinement will help define the complex challenge of assembling a population health management system to deliver care in a community.

Conceptualizing the delivery system as a population health organization is the first step toward improving health and quality of care while bringing medical cost trends in line with other economic indicators.

Medicine is a complex business, and some processes are rigid by design. But there are still simple ways to make a difference in the lives of your patients, and *population health management* is one of them. The term refers to a patient population, but in reality, it's a group of your patients — the people you see in your waiting rooms and talk with in the examination rooms. You can make a difference in their lives by assessing and changing processes.

The *2013 WEDI Report*[7] by the Workgroup for Electronic Data Interchange includes 10 recommendations to increase the effectiveness and efficiency of our healthcare system. Here are four representative examples:

1. Patient engagement — identifying ways to enable patient engagement through improved electronic access to critical healthcare information;

2. Payment models — identifying business, information, and data exchange requirements that will help enable emerging payment models;

3. Data harmonization and exchange — identifying ways to better align administrative and clinical information capture, linkage, and exchange; and

4. Innovative patient encounter models — identifying business cases for innovative encounter models that use existing and emergent technologies.

These elements of the report touch on the quality management domain because they refer to changes to administrative processes that affect patient care. They help eliminate wasteful administrative processes that detract from high-quality patient care and help practices focus on their true mission of supporting the delivery of high-quality patient care.

Patient-Centered Medical Home

The goal of a patient-centered medical home (PCMH) delivery model is to ensure that patients have consistent relationships with their healthcare providers. In the traditional healthcare model, a patient presented a complaint a few times a year and the physician reacted to it. In the new model, patients are expected to be actively involved in their healthcare and the medical practice helps the patient make better choices year-round.

The model is based on the fact that patients might only be in a medical practice for a few hours each year, but tend to base all of their health outcomes and accountability on those few brief visits. PCMH recognizes that patients are responsible for their own healthcare for 8,740 or more of the 8,760 hours in a year, and uses tools that make it clear that patients are ultimately responsible for most of their own care.

One way to implement the PCMH model is to organize clinic staff members into primary care manager (PCM) teams that are designed to reinforce communication between patient and provider, optimize continuity of care, and provide accountability. Each team could, for example, consist of one physician, a physician assistant or nurse practitioner, a nurse, and five medical technicians.

You should talk with people at other practices who use the PCMH model to see if they can provide guidance on the:

- Requirements to operate as a medical home;

- Infrastructure, teams, and workflow to support the operations;

- Measures of performance for the model, such as PCM continuity of care, appointment availability, patient satisfaction, urgent and emergency care utilization, and several of the Healthcare Effectiveness Data and Information Set (HEDIS) and process-improvement initiatives;

- Shared communication plans for staff and patients that outline PCMH benefits; and

- Continuous access to coaches before, during, and after PCMH implementation.

When the PCMH model is in place, steps should be taken to measure:

- Continuity of care;

- Emergency and urgent care utilization rates;

- HEDIS; and

- Patient satisfaction.

One main advantage of the PCMH delivery model is that if it is properly set up, it can provide patients with more comprehensive medical care and support without affecting the productivity of physicians, physician assistants, and nurse practitioners. For example, instead of trying to accomplish everything needed in a 15-minute appointment window, a PCMH model uses a team-based approach where a medical assistant spends 15 minutes preparing patients for their visit and a nurse spends 15 minutes educating patients after their visit, giving patients 45 minutes of quality healthcare.

It is also critical to communicate with patients throughout the year, giving them the tools, feedback, and support they need to responsibly manage their own healthcare. Use the telephone, e-mail, and mail to actively engage with patients and help monitor data that can be used to spot trends and proactively intervene.

Accountable Care

ACOs are touted as the future of healthcare; and whether they flourish or falter, there is no question that practice executives must be skilled at measuring the four cornerstones of accountable care:

1. Safety;

2. Quality;

3. Cost-effectiveness; and

4. Patient satisfaction.

The fifth element that is also critical to a practice's ability to deliver accountable care is staff satisfaction, and that includes physicians. Like psychologist Abraham Maslow's hierarchy of needs, which suggests people are motivated by unsatisfied needs and that certain lower needs must be satisfied before higher needs can be addressed, it is virtually impossible to focus on the altruism of accountable care if staff members are dissatisfied with their work.[8]

A question that often goes unaddressed is to whom are medical practices accountable? While the primary answer is patients, you must answer to other constituencies. The general public as well as payers, both public and private, want assurance that your organization is delivering safe, high-quality, cost-effective care. There is a time in the not-too-distant future where the public will have access to metrics for comparing providers to whom they might entrust their care.

There are many performance metrics in place to measure the cornerstones of safety, quality, cost-effectiveness, and satisfaction. Clearly, payment based on performance lies just around the corner. Smart practice executives will establish applicable measures in their practices and begin benchmarking them (internally and externally) to improve organizational performance.

Because no healthcare provider is an island, and success under the ACO paradigm will require providers to work together, expect to see more integration in the coming years. Physicians should be leaders, not followers, in this trend. To do this, it is important to focus on the following four key concepts:

1. **A changing set of competencies for practice executives.** All of us will need new skills to succeed in our jobs. Whether your group stands alone or integrates with a larger system, practice executives will need to update their core competencies. Professionals in stand-alone practices will spend more time managing relationships and components of accountable care in larger systems. Those integrating with a larger system will need to update competencies to remain a vital component of the system.

2. **A different measure of success.** Regardless of organization type, practices will be measured by a different yardstick. The old days of using physician productivity as the measure of practice success and the basis for physician compensation are not likely to continue. With methods of reimbursement such as gain sharing, payment bundling, and capitation, success will be measured — and physicians compensated — in different ways. Determining the appropriate metrics or systems and ensuring provider satisfaction under the new rules will be the responsibility of practice executives who will need new tools to manage this transition successfully.

3. **The diversity challenge.** Whether practices remain independent or integrate, professionals will need to interface systems in different ways. Even stand-alone practices will need to know how to integrate billing and patient record systems to coordinate care and obtain reimbursement under the new systems.

4. **A new way for physicians to work.** Physicians will be driven by the new payment systems to assume more risk for the overall health of patient populations. As such, they will be driven

into a more transparent relationship with patients focused on wellness, which leads to different measures of productivity and success. Healthcare administrators will not only develop these systems but manage their physicians through these changes. They will need exceptional change management and leadership skills to navigate this process.

::: Conclusion

The practice executive's role in the delivery of patient-centered care continues to evolve. A more concentrated focused on improving patient experience and quality outcomes and improving health outcomes of a population while at the same time reducing costs has necessitated the practice executive's involvement in certain aspects of the care delivery process. Shared vision, defined roles, and consistent communication with providers and staff is the best strategy to provide excellent patient-centered care.

Value-based care programs and contracting are becoming part of the practice administrator's everyday vocabulary. The reporting requirements in value-based care programs have evolved beyond simply reporting patient visits. Now it's about all patient *touches* and meaningful use measures, such as access to patient portals and e-mail contact with physicians. There are also clinical requirements, such as which screenings have been completed, whether the practice has contacted patients who are overdue for exams, tracking calls and letters to patients, follow-up contacts, referrals, surgeries, and hospital readmissions. Designing, implementing, tracking, and maintaining quality metrics and activities are integral in patient-centered care.

Notes

1. Brian Mathwich, "Using the Process Map to Improve Your Bottom Line," *MGMA Connexion* 4, no. 6 (2004): 31.
2. Elizabeth Woodcock, *Mastering Patient Flow*, 4th ed. (Englewood, CO: Medical Group Management Association, 2014), 100.
3. Stephanie J. Lee, Anthony L. Back, Susan D. Block, and Susan K. Stewart, "Enhancing Physician-Patient Communication," *Hematology: American*

Society of Hematology Education Program, (2002): 464–483, http://ash
educationbook.hematologylibrary.org/content/2002/1/464.long.

4. "Telehealth," U.S. Department of Health and Human Services, Health
Resources and Services Administration (HRSA), Rural Health, Nov. 20,
2012, www.hrsa.gov/ruralhealth/about/telehealth/.

5. © 2008 Englewood Orthopedic Associates. Reprinted with permission.

6. "Clinical Pathways," OpenClinical, modified July 8, 2015, www.open
clinical.org/clinicalpathways.html.

7. Workgroup for Electronic Data Interchange (WEDI) Foundation, *2013
WEDI Report*, 2013, www.wedi.org/topics/2013-wedi-report.

8. "Maslow's Theory of Motivation: Hierarchy of Needs," www.envision
software.com/articles/Maslows_Needs_Hierarchy.html.

Chapter 4

Quality Initiatives and Measurement

⠿ Creating and Implementing Quality Criteria

In the past, organizing for delivery of quality was not a central theme for the medical group. Many structural and operational considerations took precedence over quality of care because quality was taken for granted. The lack of standardization, absence of any formal adherence to best practices, and dearth of formalized quality improvement for programs all contributed to a failure of progress in this area.

Medical group structures are often not designed to facilitate quality initiatives. The short-term focus on financial performance is a chief culprit. Groups do not invest enough, either financially or in the training needed to conduct large-scale improvement initiatives. Investment dollars come only from the shareholders' pockets, a prospect that has long curtailed the development of modern medical groups. In his book *Out of the Crisis*, W. Edwards Deming asks a question that should serve as the cornerstone of any group's quality initiative: "What are you doing about the quality that you hope to provide to your customers four years from now?"[1]

The issue of quality in the U.S. healthcare system is becoming increasingly important as we gain more understanding about it. For most of history, quality has been virtually undefined. As Plato might have said, "Quality is in the eye of the beholder." However, that is changing dramatically and will continue to do so as measures and expectations of healthcare service quality continue to evolve.

If you've heard a lot about value-based payment contracts but have yet to actually see one, you're not alone. Although more common than they used to be, these models are not exactly ubiquitous — at least not yet. But that could change in a hurry. *Health Plan Readiness to Operationalize Value-Based Payment Models*,[2] an April 2013 research study by the health information network Availity, notes that "only 20 percent of health plan respondents say that value-based models support more than half of their business today." However, 40 percent predicted that the models would support more than 50 percent of their business in three years, and 60 percent said that would be the case in five years.

Availity defines *value-based payment plans* as "arrangements that reward physicians, hospitals, medical groups and other healthcare providers on measures including quality, efficiency and positive patient experience,"[3] and cites as examples accountable care organizations, patient-centered medical homes, payment for coordinated care, pay for performance, and bundled payments.

Many value-based programs use the National Committee for Quality Assurance Healthcare Effectiveness Data and Information Set measures as a baseline.[4] You can consult the National Quality Forum's Alignment Tool[5] to compare measures by payer and program.

Quality management is used to reduce errors and improve patient care. Knowing that patient experience influences outcomes, we are inherently motivated to reassess processes that enhance care delivery, and we find that these efforts increase provider satisfaction and improve practice culture. It starts with quality management processes and rolls outward.

Quality management initiatives help professionals design, implement, and maintain quality initiatives, measurement activities, and administrative policies and procedures that ensure patient safety and the consistent delivery of quality care. In practical terms, that means:

- Using analytical processes, such as Lean or total quality improvement programs, to improve interaction and communication between clinical teams;

- Creating internal tracking so that medical practice groups can compare their practices with others on quality, safety, and cost benchmarks; and

- Establishing, evaluating, and enforcing standards for quality.

Examples range from something as simple as taking a new approach toward enforcing hand-washing requirements to a complex retooling of referral processes for reducing patient scheduling wait times. No area should be neglected, because the return on investment from financial and emotional standpoints is powerful. Practices benefit from increased productivity and improved patient outcomes, increased physician buy-in, and enhanced partnerships for administrators and providers. As you reassess your processes, it is important to ask, "Is this the type of care that I'd want for my family member?" Working toward that goal lets your practice set a new standard for care delivery and encourages everyone to be proud of the work they do.

Implementing Changes

The first step in implementing changes is to schedule a meeting of the important stakeholders to envision how a practice wants to deliver care. The number of team members and their level of involvement will vary with each organization based on its management style, culture, size and structure, and where and how the changes are to be implemented. Team representatives could include an administrator, a physician, a clinician, and information technology (IT) and administrative support. Your team can then assess how the practice operates and ask pertinent questions, some of which might be:

- Does the practice have an efficient electronic health record (EHR) system?

- How does the staff manage supplies?

- How does the staff run labs?

- Where are computers needed?

- Is it preferable to have registration at a kiosk or a station?

Once executive leadership and the stakeholder team buy in to the concept, the change process begins, including determining and designing models. Through the process, your practice can:

- Reduce capital requirements;
- Establish a consistent model of care and optimize its delivery;
- Create a consistent, quality patient experience;
- Develop efficient, flexible environments;
- Set group purchasing standards;
- Optimize the flow of space and processes;
- Support and solidify recognizable brand identity;
- Effectively implement and integrate technology;
- Improve staff interaction; and
- Gain efficiencies throughout the practice.

It is important to standardize but with flexibility, adaptability, replicability, and modular capability.

Physician Involvement

Physician involvement and engagement in designing and implementing clinical quality programs is crucial for the success of those programs. To increase physician investment, consider creating a committee of physicians who establish a vision for the program and meet monthly to develop quality metrics. Developing a program that rewards physicians for achieving quality metrics can also help. And you will need to develop a method for capturing and analyzing those metrics, preferably one that is integrated with the EHR system you already use. If that is not possible, consider contracting a programmer or IT firm that can help you develop a metrics tracking system that is as automated as possible.

Whatever system you implement, make sure it remains relevant by having the physician committee perform a comprehensive review of your metrics at least once per year. Prune the ones that are useless, revise existing ones based on your experience with them, and add new ones based on the evolving needs of your practice.

⠿ Establishing Benchmark Targets

To determine where a practice falls with the metrics they are reporting and measuring, a baseline assessment and correlation to benchmarks needs to be done. A baseline assessment examines how well the practice is doing over the course of time compared to itself and external practices.

Why Benchmark?

Benchmarking permits medical practices to accomplish five important goals:

1. **It facilitates understanding of the performance of key processes and performance outcomes.** This has to do with the concept of measurement. With measurement, medical practice executives are able to better understand the performance of their medical practices.

2. **It permits healthcare leaders to view the performance of their own practices over time.** One of the most important concepts of benchmarking is to understand whether or not performance is improving or deteriorating. If a decision is made to change staffing levels or the staffing model, what results are expected? A time series benchmark — a before measure and an after measure — is needed that reflects the performance of the practice before the intervention so that medical practice executives are able to evaluate the positive or perhaps even the negative aspects of that intervention.

3. **It permits comparison of measurements against peer groups.** Measurements include average comparisons as well as comparisons with organizations that exhibit higher levels of performance — organizations that are considered better performing medical practices.

4. **It provides an opportunity to analyze the processes of others to understand what they do differently.** Some organizations benchmark their activity to organizations outside of their own industry to determine if there are innovative opportunities that have not been considered and to better understand how they want to do business. For example, a medical practice executive may want to examine the processing of accounts in the banking industry to facilitate better understanding of the physician billing process or accounts payable process. They may also want to examine the hotel industry to learn of opportunities to enhance

patient satisfaction. Medical practice executives may want to look at many other industries that are not involved in healthcare and may apply innovative, creative ideas learned to their own medical practices (and in the process perhaps even become a best practice for others to emulate).

5. **It is used to convince others of the need for change.** At times, healthcare leaders find themselves in positions where they need to convince administrators, physicians, nonphysician providers, managers, supervisors, support staff, and others that change is needed. Benchmarking the current state of the medical practice against other practices can often assist in moving the organization forward or better positioning the organization to achieve its strategic goals, because it provides a clear and simple picture of the practice's current strengths and shortcomings.

Using Data Analytics as an Assessment Tool

Data analytics is simply a new term to describe what medical office administrators and other business professionals have done for years: Compile practice data for internal and external analysis, create action plans to bolster vulnerable areas, and create incentives for staff members to embrace new approaches.

You just read about benchmarking, but to use that data to identify strengths and weaknesses in a medical practice, you need a basic assessment that includes:

- Overall practice performance;
- Physician productivity;
- Ancillary service productivity; and
- Billing department efficiency.

Administrators can identify problems and develop corrective action plans by using data from their practices to identify problems and guide corrective action planning. Use raw data to uncover benchmarks for overall performance. Then use year-to-year comparisons to help provide an internal analysis. For example, if net revenues improve over time and overhead decreases over the same period, it means the group is heading in a positive direction or has a positive trend.

Use the results of the internal analysis to guide a corrective action plan. For example, let's say you discover that physician productivity is low and the billing department is inefficient. To address the former issue, you could implement a more efficient scheduling process and invest in marketing and referring physician outreach to bring in more patients. Billing inefficiency could be caused by a poor third-party provider, which might prompt switching to a different provider or creating an in-house billing department. You can use the same benchmarks and analytics you created to develop an action plan to monitor the success of that action plan.

The data analysis process is the same for every type of medical group and all types of businesses. Follow the data to identify the problem and design a solution to repair it. Using a more detailed form of this process will reveal strengths and weaknesses of every department in a practice. In the beginning, focus the data analysis on key indicators used in the Medical Group Management Association® (MGMA®) *Performance and Practices of Successful Medical Groups* report[6] to provide a solid foundation for practice analysis.

Compile the data in an annual report for shareholders and you will demonstrate a firm grasp of your practice's status and have the ability to make accurate projections of future performance. Instituting a program that links performance measures to rewards will help ensure staff buy-in for these kinds of action plans.

Patient Satisfaction

Patient satisfaction is a great quality initiative that can be used to demonstrate how benchmark targets can be obtained and used. Patient satisfaction measurement tools can provide great feedback for areas in which improvement in quality of processes can be applied, and where staff training on communication and interaction with patients and families will improve the overall relationship of the practice to its customers, patients, and families.

The goal of gathering data is to use it to make change. Patient satisfaction data are useless, however, unless they are used. Properly analyzed, such data hold the key to patient retention and reduced likelihood of litigation. Whatever the methods used by the organization to gather information about patient satisfaction, they should be used to spur change and pinpoint areas for improvement on an ongoing basis

There is no way to guess if your patients believe they are receiving satisfactory care and being treated properly when they visit your office. It takes planning and assessment to get meaningful feedback and to fine-tune your office so patients receive the best possible care, feel valued, and advocate for your practice. Feedback can take many forms:

- **A patient survey** conducted at regular intervals and designed to provide relevant feedback from the patients' perspective;

- **Mystery patient assessments**, in which experienced professionals probe beyond the survey data to evaluate the specific performance dimensions that affect patient satisfaction;

- **Key-person interviews** to obtain input from the physicians and employees who work directly with patients and have the best ideas on how to improve service levels; and

- **Related performance indicators** that affect patient satisfaction, including staff turnover rates, requests for records transfer, trends in referrals from other physicians, anecdotal patient complaints, malpractice claims, and other data that measure the service strengths and weaknesses of the practice.

⠿ Evaluating Performance

A goal of patient care is to provide the best care and just the right amount of it. Quality management and utilization management processes within the practice have tremendous effect on the cost of services and the outcomes. Triggers for quality management should include any of the exposures in patient care identified during the quality assessment. Each is a potential quality area where patient care is compromised. Furthermore, standard triggers for quality review include sentinel events, repeat admissions within 30 days, and healthcare-acquired infections, among others. Issues of quality are identified in many ways. Standard event reports and patient complaints are sources of quality information. Furthermore, billing denials and attorney letters of inquiry provide clues to issues of utilization or quality care. Quality improvement should not be a reactive function in post-problem identification, but rather a proactive part of the quality management process to identify problems before they become events.

For quality to be an integral part of the care process, staff members must be trained to recognize and report both actual events and situations where systems or processes result in compromised patient safety or care. The organization must have an infrastructure that supports ongoing process improvement through dedicated staff members who are trained in process improvement techniques, including root cause analysis and failure modes and effects analysis, as well as through resources for making and monitoring recommended changes.

Utilization management ties into the quality process through monitoring practice patterns, patient visits, and admissions. Outlier practice patterns, variation in service patterns, and changes in admission and discharge patterns are all indicators of potential quality or process concerns.

⠿ Quality Assurance Programs

In addition to determining and implementing the appropriate quality initiatives and benchmarks, an organization should create and administer a variety of quality assurance programs to measure the results of the quality initiative implementation and ensure that the desired goals are being reached. Most quality assurance programs can be sized to meet the needs of both large and small medical practices. Depending on the size of the organization, some practices complete their quality assurance programs internally whereas other practices use outside consultants to complete the necessary reviews, audits, and surveys.

A key tool in evaluating adherence to appropriate quality initiatives and benchmarks and their effect on the patient population is through the use of various outcomes measures, including chart reviews, where a sample of medical records is reviewed to confirm that the proper care is being provided and properly documented. Other measurements include patient and referring-physician satisfaction surveys. These surveys, when completed properly and analyzed in a timely manner, can provide a wealth of information concerning how well the clinical pathways are being received and whether the pathways are in keeping with the standards in the community and the expectations of the patient. The results of these reviews and surveys should be presented to senior clinical and administrative management to enable them to address the issues raised by the results of the surveys and reviews.

The data used to define the issues may be perceived differently when reviewed by clinical and administrative staff members. Clinicians will be primarily seeking to improve the care being provided to enable the patient to reach the best possible outcome. This goal is important from the administrative point of review as well, but the medical practice administrator is also concerned that the care and service are being provided in the most cost-effective manner with the most efficient use of available resources. Finally, these data are critical to identifying and determining modifications that need to be made in both the strategic and operational planning processes.

::: Feedback and Corrective Action

All businesses live or die by their processes, and developing a program to consistently improve those processes is needed to achieve sustainable growth, account for changes in the external environment, and keep up with changes within the business itself. The practice that does not constantly test its own organization's core processes and develop and implement ways to improve the operation will stagnate and eventually be unable to meet the clinical and business challenges of the future. The key knowledge and skills necessary to effectively manage the process improvement efforts of a medical practice include identifying organizational needs and desired outcomes, applying quality assessment techniques, developing policies and procedures, enforcing corrective action, and establishing continuous process improvement review.

Process improvement means challenging the way that things have always been done. Not all process improvement programs will meet their goals, but all will produce a positive gain for organizations willing to take some risk to improve themselves. Through the use of audits, outside reviews, compliance reviews, and just standing back and asking "Why do we do this process this way?" an organization can identify the key areas where improvements in the operation and sustainability of the practice can be made. Process improvement also requires an investment of time and thought to evaluate a system and determine a better way to do the job and an investment in education and training so employees learn new processes, leaders can implement them, and their outcomes can be monitored and evaluated.

In the realm of clinical practice, areas for review that may result in process improvement include coding documentation, risk assessments, chart audits, and auditing of compliance with regulatory and payer regulations. Within these areas, specific types of audits, reviews, and assessments can include:

- Reviewing medical records to evaluate completeness of documentation and to identify those providers whose documentation either does not support the procedural or visit code used or who are using a procedural or visit code that is lower than the documentation can support;

- Determining if the diagnosis coding has the highest level of specificity that matches the clinical documentation;

- Comparing the compliance requirements of the various regulatory agencies and third-party payers that use guidelines and policies to ensure that the practice meets the expectations and coverage determinations for medical necessity of these outside entities; and

- Reviewing and analyzing the historical data of the organization (e.g., malpractice claims, patient complaints, and external evaluations) to identify trends and areas for additional review and analysis.

All of these reviews can be used as part of larger outcome-based quality assurance programs, which in turn give rise to and support many process improvement initiatives. Structures, processes, and outcomes are the vital components of a quality assurance program and provide the operational focus for it.

Clearly, no one method of measurement has yet evolved as a gold standard. In most cases, these areas are first addressed through the use of the various audits and assessments. Within larger organizations, these audits can be done internally, assuming qualified personnel exist within the practice. In other cases, these reviews can be contracted out to qualified consultants who can provide the same data to the practice.

The findings, which reflect on the current structure, process, and outcomes of the services of the organization, are often presented to senior clinical and administrative management for review and corrective action. Without proper and effective communication to all stakeholders, the value of these findings is greatly diminished. To be most effective, communication of these findings should be provided in written format, but within the context of a face-to-face meeting where discussion can take place.

These findings, if used properly, become the basis for implementing the various methodologies that may be applied to improve the processes within the organization, including:

1. Flowcharting the process being reviewed to identify possible redundancies or dead ends within the process;

2. Reviewing historical data that may exist from previous assessments, such as chart audits, coding reviews, and assessments, and comparing those data to current data to identify variations and possible trends that will spotlight concerns and issues; and

3. Completing surveys of patient, referring physician, and employee satisfaction levels to identify issues of concern to these groups of stakeholders.

These methodologies are useful in identifying issues, areas for improvement, and possible systemic changes related to the processes in effect. It is often advisable to implement pilot programs before executing changes on an organization-wide basis. Through application on a limited scale, an organization is able to test the proposed changes to ensure that there are no unanticipated ramifications. After these changes are proven through a pilot program, they can be applied safely throughout the organization.

To properly apply and maximize the effect of these reviews within the organization, it is necessary to create teaching models and techniques that effectively impart this knowledge to the staff of the organization. These models vary significantly, based on several factors, including the size of the organization, existing staff mix, complexity of the changes that are being envisioned, and amount of time that can be made available for training and education purposes.

In small organizations, this training can consist of staff meetings with senior physicians and management providing the training through the use of lectures and roundtable discussions. In larger practices, this training and education may be expanded to include department-specific classes, use of online training and outside consultants or vendors, and sending staff members to off-site courses and seminars. Without this training and support from senior management and physicians, it is difficult or even impossible to obtain staff buy-in to these new process improvements. It is through this investment in time and resources that an organization will be able to realize improvements in their processes and clinical outcomes.

⠿ Conclusion

The practice executive's role in the delivery of patient-centered care continues to evolve. Value-based contracts that emphasize quality metrics, patient experience, and reduced costs have necessitated the practice executive's involvement in certain aspects of the care delivery process. Shared vision, defined roles, and consistent communication with providers and staff members is the best strategy to provide excellent patient-centered care.

Notes

1. W. Edwards Deming, *Out of the Crisis* (Cambridge, MA: Massachusetts Institute of Technology, Center for Advanced Engineering Studies, 1990), 166.

2. *Health Plan Readiness to Operationalize Value-Based Payment Models* (An Availity Research Study), Availity, April 2013, www.nbch.org/nbch/files/ccLibraryFiles/Filename/000000002854/Availity_Study_on_Plan_Readiness_to_Operationalize_New_Payt_Models.pdf.

3. *Health Plan Readiness to Operationalize Value-Based Payment Models*.

4. "HEDIS Measures," National Committee for Quality Assurance (NCQA) Healthcare Effectiveness Data and Information Set (HEDIS), www.ncqa.org/HEDISQualityMeasurement/HEDISMeasures.aspx.

5. "Community Tool to Align Measurement," National Quality Forum, www.qualityforum.org/alignmenttool/.

6. MGMA, *Performance and Practices of Successful Medical Groups: 2014 Report Based on 2013 Data* (Englewood, CO: Medical Group Management Association, 2014).

Resource List

::: Organizational Governance Resources

The following resources are available on the Medical Group Management Association® (MGMA®) Website. Please visit the MGMA Store at www.mgma.org/store for updates and new products. Members of MGMA seeking assistance locating articles and industry resources on organizational governance may contact the MGMA Knowledge Center at infocenter@mgma.org.

MGMA Books

- *Leadership Strategies: Achieving Personal and Professional Success*, by Ronald Menaker (2013). Item # 8707.
- *Physician Policies: A Practical Guide to Governance Issues*, by Marshall M. Baker and Kenneth M. Hekman (2011). Item # 8260.

MGMA Practice Resources Topics and Tools Sections

See the following topic-focused sections on the MGMA Website:

- Governance and Leadership
- Organizational Governance Tools
  - Physician Retirement and Practice Transition Self-Assessment
  - Compensation System Self-Assessment

   – Integrated System Performance Self-Assessment
   – Strategic Planning Self-Assessment

MGMA Connection Magazine — Organizational Governance Focus

- *Organizational Governance* issue, published each November/ December, is an array of articles that drill down into specific Body of Knowledge domain topics.
- *Medical Practice Today*, published each July, is a review of the annually updated "What Members Have to Say" research, focusing on challenges faced by MGMA members and what they're doing to survive and thrive in today's healthcare environment.
- *The State of Medical Practice*, published each January, is an annual update to the myriad issues medical practice executives will grapple with in the coming year.

MGMA Education — Self-Study Course

- Essentials of Organizational Governance

⠿ Patient-Centered Care Resources

The following resources are available on the MGMA Website. Members of MGMA seeking assistance locating articles and industry resources on patient-centered care may contact the MGMA Knowledge Center at infocenter@mgma.org.

MGMA Books and Reports

- *A Comparison of the National Patient-Centered Medical Home Accreditation and Recognition Programs*, by David N. Gans (2014). Electronic download, Item # E8789.

- *Front Office Success: How to Satisfy Patients and Boost the Bottom Line*, by Elizabeth W. Woodcock (2011). Item # 8253. DVD format, Item # 8547.

- *It's Your Call: Mastering the Telephones in Your Medical Practice*, by Elizabeth W. Woodcock and Deborah Walker-Keegan (2013). Item # 8596.

- *Mastering Patient Flow*, by Elizabeth W. Woodcock (2014). Item # 8780. Electronic download, Item # E8806.

- *PCMH Policies & Procedures Guidebook*, by Elizabeth W. Woodcock (2014). eBook, Item # E8807.

- *PCSP (Patient-Centered Specialty Practice) Policies & Procedures Guidebook*, by Elizabeth W. Woodcock (2014). eBook, Item # E8808.

- *Star-Studded Service: Six Steps to Winning Patient Satisfaction, 2nd edition*, by Kevin W. Sullivan, Meryl D. Luallin, and MGMA (2011). Item # 8595.

MGMA Practice Resources Topics and Tools Sections

See the following topic-focused sections on the MGMA Website:
- Patient Care Delivery
- Patient Care Systems Tools

- Patient Flow
- Quality Management

MGMA Connection Magazine — Patient-Centered Care Focus

- *Business of Care Delivery* is a special supplement.
- *Medical Practice Today*, published each July, is a review of the annually updated "What Members Have to Say" research, focusing on challenges faced by MGMA members and what they're doing to survive and thrive in today's healthcare environment.
- *Patient Care* issue, published each March, is an array of articles that drill down into specific Body of Knowledge domain topics.
- *Ripple Effects: From Process to Patient Care* is a special supplement.
- *The State of Medical Practice*, published each January, is an annual update to the myriad issues medical practice executives will grapple with in the coming year.

MGMA Education — Online Course

- Essentials of Patient Centered Care

Index

NOTE: *ex.* indicates exhibit.

CPSIA information can be obtained
at www.ICGtesting.com
Printed in the USA
FSOW02n1554150816
23612FS

9 781568 294797